THE ETHICS OF CRITICISM
AND OTHER ESSAYS.

THE
ETHICS OF CRITICISM
AND OTHER ESSAYS

BY

N. HARDY WALLIS, M.A.

KENNIKAT PRESS, INC./PORT WASHINGTON, N. Y.

To

My Mother

THE ETHICS OF CRITICISM AND OTHER ESSAYS

First published 1924
Reissued 1968 by Kennikat Press

Library of Congress Catalog Card No: 68-26289
Manufactured in the United States of America

CONTENTS.

THE ETHICS OF CRITICISM.

A Paper read before the " Gwynant " Society of Hampstead. January, 1923.

THE ETHICS OF CRITICISM.

THOSE who deprecate criticism may derive much
authority from the statement " Judge not, that ye be
not judged "; but this rule of thought must not be
taken in the literal sense, and is better translated
" Condemn not, that ye be not condemned "; for
judgment and condemnation are not the same, and
while the human mind may exercise a right to the
first action, the second should be cautious, as no
mortal estimate can be final. The virtue of criticism
lies, not so much in its result, as in its use; for it
implies a careful study of the thing criticised; and
this deliberate consideration tends to a more balanced
verdict on the subject. The philosophical mind is
essentially critical; the desire to discover " Why ? "
is an eternal human heritage. Abraham questioned
the Almighty, and his argument " Shall not the Judge
of all the earth do right ? " was logical and could
only be answered in the affirmative; Job demanded
an explanation of his sufferings, but went unsatis-
fied; Buddha sought an interpretation of the mystery
of life in self-examination, and Christ in a law of
love; as have some modern scientists, one of whom
writes " The physicist looks at the data and says,
' It is all law '; the philosopher ponders them and
concludes, 'It is all mind'; but the greatest induction
is that of the man who has lived through it all, noting
the resultant of the various sequences in the case of
his own experience, and who can truthfully say at
the end ' It was all love.' "[1] In the history of mental

(1) J. Y. Simpson. " The Spiritual Interpretation of Nature," Chap. V.

philosophy, as in that of religion, the search for enlightenment took place. Plato asked " What is the ideal ? ", and has been met with many replies, but with no accurate definition; Bacon attempted to catalogue knowledge, and, in his own words, "Mapped out the coast of the new intellectual world" on the basis " that if we begin with certainties we shall end in doubts, but if we begin with doubts, and are patient in them, we shall end in certainties".[1] The system of Descartes went deeper and was built on the noble phrase "cogito ergo sum ", while that of Kant with his "categorical imperative " emphasised the importance of the personality and the existence of the transcendent. The work of such teachers may be truly called the " higher criticism ", for it is the discussion of the greatest truths in a dispassionate and reverent manner. This is the method of accurate consideration and judgment, of unbiassed thought and careful investigation; and it is a remarkable fact that although the noblest minds have always realised the impossibility of absolute knowledge, they have none the less sought it with eagerness. This instinct of quest is the basis of all criticism, and the idealism of its end and aim, a sufficient vindication for its use. Criticism has, therefore, an ethical foundation, and may be held to be a divine faculty in man.

It is now necessary to turn from a justification of the critical faculty to its function; and in this connection the definition of Matthew Arnold may be noticed, " Criticism is a disinterested endeavour to learn and propagate the best that is known and thought in the world ".[2] The first adjective excludes all those judgments which are founded on personal

(1) Francis Bacon. " Advancement of Learning ", Bk. I. (2) Matthew Arnold. " Function of Criticism ".

admiration or dislike, for little importance may be attached to the thinker who is so convinced of the truth of his interpretation of the truth, that he will condemn that of all others in comparison. The " endeavour " implies the realisation that the task is difficult, and a desire for knowledge previous to its dissemination, necessitates an estimate and selection of the relevant from the irrelevant factors; while the concluding words require a decision as to the achievement which has been the greatest service to mankind. Theoretically, therefore, this is an entirely satisfactory definition of criticism, but practically it is doubtful if the detached attitude is either possible or even desirable. For example—Two critics of equal scholarship and information decide on the merits or defects of an action, but it does not follow that their judgments will be in agreement, for no one can entirely submerge his own personality. The endeavour may be made from as many bases as there are aspects of the subject. Two writers attempt to define the place of a poet, the one working from a conviction that his gift to the world has been an added ease of metre and expression, the other assured that the outstanding beauty of his work lies in his fresh view of the common life; and both endeavours, while entirely sincere, reflect the mind of the critic. Again, a writer of one country strives to arrive at a just appreciation of an event or production of some other, without paying sufficient regard to national characteristics. Nothing, moreover, is of greater difficulty than the weighing of information, for this is influenced by both the preceding considerations. Finally, who would be so bold as to say that what he believes to be the best, is indeed so; and to avoid this dangerous statement, refuge is taken in a consensus

of opinion. It seems, therefore, that a simpler definition than that of Arnold is necessary to guide the
seeker after a practical interpretation of criticism,
and this may be found perhaps in a comparison of
the thing criticised, in regard to its environment,
with those accepted as good by the noblest minds.
The factor of surroundings is a more powerful
influence than is often supposed, for the mental
development of humanity will alter it, and the alteration will react upon thought. Truth, although pure
as the diamond, has innumerable facets. Our present-
day judgment of Shakespeare, as a master-dramatist,
is very different from that of his contemporaries as
a play-writer; and Milton, the Latin Secretary, was
a more important person in the seventeenth century,
than Milton the epicist. Thus criticism varies with
time; it also varies with place. Little weight is given
to the verdict of the countryman on city life, or to
that of the monk on political expediency. It is the
first requisite of a critic that he should be in touch
with that which he is judging. It is not true idealism,
but a danger to reasonable estimation and appraisement when a mind is eager to condemn mankind
because it falls short of perfection. It has been
pointed out above, that the greatest intellects are
always willing to recognise that after a certain stage
of investigation, they are ignorant, and the realisation that nothing is capable of absolute proof, should
warn them from an attitude of too great dogmatism.
Invention which is so realistic as to be accepted as
fact, may indeed often lead to mistaken criticism. A
good example is furnished by the legend of the
wanderings of Henry Howard in Italy. In the year
1594, Thomas Nashe published his extraordinary tale,
" The Unfortunate Traveller ", which contained,

among many other adventures, an account of the
Earl of Surrey's journeyings in the South of Europe;
although the story was filled with anachronisms, it
was believed to be genuine by the poet Drayton, who,
in 1598, made it the subject of two of his " Heroicall
Epistles "; and by the historian Warton, who did
not refuse to accept the legend even while he guarded
himself with the words " the travels of Surrey have
the air of a romance ". The true facts were only
discovered at a much later date. The incident has
been well summarised by D'Israeli, " Thus it
happened that the romancer, on a misconception,
constructs an imaginary fabric; the poet Drayton
builds on the romancer; the sober antiquary on both;
then the commentators stand upon the antiquary ".[1]
Besides being an example of critical fallibility, this
incident is a proof of the danger of receiving facts on
the authority of another writer without confirmation,
a method adopted by many unscholarly critics.
Intemperate judgment and lack of accurate knowledge are the bane of criticism, whether it be literary,
musical, artistic or philosophical. In literature they
lead to such statements as that free verse is more
beautiful than stanzaic structure; in music that the
movement of unrest is more satisfying than simply-
flowing melody; in art that the personal impression is
more important than restraint of treatment; and in
philosophy that the conception of relativity is entirely
new. To say this is not to condemn the modern
writer, musician, artist or philosopher, but only to
urge the development of a greater sense of proportion
between past reticence and present free expression.
Because the new is of great interest and fascination,
it is not necessary to entirely neglect the old. Surely

(1) " Amenities of Literature." The Earl of Surrey and Sir Thomas Wyatt.

this very interest and fascination depend on the contrast with the past. Criticism must advance with time and keep in touch with the present, but there have been great characters and events in history which cannot be forgotten. Perhaps many modernists would like to forget to remember for fear of rivalry. Is this possible in this self-confident age! It is said sometimes that our era of self-assertion has no great men. Granted that the general standard of culture is higher than it has ever been before, it is not a just verdict, for the tendency towards specialisation has driven the thinker of to-day into certain paths of thought, and it is absurd for any mind to repeat the affirmation of Bacon, " I have taken all knowledge to be my province ".[1] There are, however, great leaders and followers advancing over every road to truth. Criticism is bound to be more limited in scope, but it can be more thorough. A factor tending to lessen a careful estimate is the modern desire for summarised knowledge on a topic. The critic who can compress world-history into a volume, or an intelligent appraisement of Shakespeare into a monograph, is welcome, but most liable to the sin of superficiality. On the other hand, this age has not time for the many-tomed exposition of a view or of a theory. It is a remarkable fact that, in an era of specialisation, there should be so many little books on great subjects. There are two possible explanations. The quantity of research required for the adequate knowledge of a particular subject is very large, and allows but small time for the consideration of extraneous matters, however interesting. The desire to be slightly acquainted with several subjects rather than to know much about one. It is the function of criticism to

(1) Bacon. Letter to Lord Burleigh.

hold the scales between the trifler and the scholar. At this point it may be brought forward that criticism is a collection of judgments and cannot take up an impartial position as an agent in the solution of the problem. This is quite true, but the average opinion should have some authority. A work is produced— the scholars study and eulogise or condemn it, while the multitude take no notice; the critics, however, if really worthy of their name, are aware that there is over-emphasis on one, and undue neglect on the other side; for the first attach unfair weight to research and technicality; blaming those who will not recognise them; while the second ignorantly think them to be wasting time on futile labours. Here is another aspect of criticism. And there is also a third, which embraces the two preceding. No appreciation nor depreciation of a character or act but produces a reciprocal condemnation or support; so that there is no universal tribunal with the power to establish its decree. Because it is omnipresent, criticism must be relative. If " Poetry be a criticism of Life " then Life must be a criticism of Poetry. In a desire to set up some definite standard, academies were formed, but before long there were as many brilliant brains outside as within their ranks. Thought is unconfinable by any particular organisation, for if captured it will always escape to make a critical attack on its previous prison. It must be recognised as universal.

It may well seem that the definition given earlier in this study, " Criticism is a comparison of the thing criticised, in relation to its environment, with those accepted as good by the noblest minds " has been forgotten. This, however, is not so, as the previous pages are an endeavour to show the dangers of unconsidered application of critical standards, and some true uses of the faculty. They may be summarised as follows. The risks are, lack of historical perspective and of contact with the subject, non-realisation of progressive development, insufficiency of study and intemperance of judgment; the advantages, or rather the desirable functions, are correct estimation of the merits of student and dilettante, of scholar and public, and a conception of the universality of knowledge and its relative application. The standard of criticism will depend on the balance of these opposing forces.

As an example of the true critical method in practice, the case of a newly discovered papyrus of some additional " *logia* " may be taken. The finder, who will probably be an archæologist, will recognise the antiquity and value of the treasure, but at the same time be on his guard against forgery; he will compare it carefully with other similar discoveries and expert opinion on them. The pith will then reach the hands of the scholar, who will endeavour to translate it and estimate its merit, authenticity and date, contrasting it with others of which he has detailed knowledge from the researches of earlier and contemporary authorities. After this he will, in all probability, have a facsimile with an accompanying version prepared and published, depositing the original in some Museum. The reproduction will be welcomed by societies interested in Egyptology, Palæography and Religious Thought; the first on account of its age and place of discovery, the second on account of its language and script, and the third for its ethical teaching or additional information. So far, the papyrus has been in the keeping of experts, but before long a Press notice or review brings it to the eyes of the public, who expect instruction without

technicality and information without boredom. The
writer, therefore, will need the faculty of selection.
Finally, those who do not happen to read the paper
containing the account of the discovery and of the
" *logia* ", will either hear of it in conversation or
remain ignorant of its existence. All, save the last
mentioned, are critics. The discoverer criticises the
place, age, and genuineness of his find, the scholar
its significance and meaning, the society its value as
a treasure, the reviewer how far it will interest the
public, and, finally, the reader how important it may
be to his intellectual life. In theory this consensus
of criticism should be in every way both sincere and
productive of fresh thought and desire for knowledge,
but in practice this effect will not be attained. The
archæologist and palæographer will most probably
undertake further researches, and the Societies support their continued endeavour; but the writer who
introduces the matter to the public will not wish,
even if he had the time, to become an authority on
the subject however he may appreciate the new
information given to the world, nor will the reader,
unless it strikes in him a responsive chord, care to
pursue the topic further. Yet it would not be fair
to condemn as mere dilettanti the reviewer and the
reader, the former supplying that which the latter
demands; for, although they may not be inspired
with a devotion to this particular subject, they will
both realise that in an addition to knowledge there
is always beauty and use, directing their critical
faculties to a decision on its value to mankind.

It is now time to collect the scattered reflections
of this study into a single beam, and, if possible, to
discover an ethical basis and practical criterion of
criticism. In its widest sense the rule may be stated

as a realisation that thought is universal and progressive, that judgment reaches its highest faculty when it can rightly estimate what is relevant or impertinent to the advance of knowledge, and an acknowledgment that there is no absolutely conclusive proof. In its application and practice, critical appraisement becomes a comparison of new work with the best which has been achieved in the particular direction by other workers, past and contemporary, necessitates scholarship and care, and should lead to fresh endeavour and achievement. Both interpretations require the exercise of selective skill, which may be held to be the highest common factor in the sum of criticism. Its ethics, therefore, are those of selection, already mentioned, perception of sequence, depth of information, clarity of vision, temperance of judgment; and, above all, a recognition of the mobile state of all standards save that of Truth; Truth to the laws of Nature, Truth to the highest ideals of man. Critics must differ if they are honest, for no human minds are identical, but it is on their combined estimations that the world must accept or refuse a thought or work. Reasonable thought, sincerely critical, concerning the Universe, will always leave fresh fields for discovery, yet will never disappoint the thinker, for he will find omnipresent, the immortal laws of Truth and of Love, the eternal manifestations of God.

TWO MODERN PLAYS ON
SHAKESPEARE.

NOTE.

The Manuscript of this Study has been submitted to the respective authors who have sanctioned its publication.

" Shakespeare ". A Play in Five Episodes. By H. F. Rubinstein and Clifford Bax. With a preface by A. W. Pollard. London, Benn Brothers, Ltd. 1921.

" Will Shakespeare ". An Invention in Four Acts. By Clemence Dane. Heinemann, London. 1921.

TWO MODERN PLAYS ON
SHAKESPEARE.

IT is always of interest to compare the modern and the contemporary estimates of a famous writer. The former, founded on a large quantity of biographical and literary material, will give a portrait of the author and his work; but the latter a picture of the actual man as he appeared to his age. The view of posterity is approximately complete, that of the time but partial, yet both are of the greatest value in a critical appraisement. It may seem a strange paradox, but it is largely true to say that the greater the writer, the less he is revealed to us in the words or works of his fellow-authors: in English Literature, for instance, we have few contemporary references to Shakespeare, but many to Ben Jonson. Two explanations of this may be brought forward. The first is that genius is always in advance of and above its own age, and is therefore less appreciated by it than would be just; the second, that the creative temperament is apt to be reticent concerning its moments of highest inspiration, and for this reason will be of less interest to contemporaries. The two poets above mentioned are excellent examples of this. Shakespeare cared little, so we may suppose, for the verdict of his time, save in so far as he realised that the dramatic force of his plays would appeal to his audience, and was probably aware that many of his finest soliloquies were above and beyond them; Jonson, anxious to be hailed as the dramatist of his time, discussed " Everyman in and out of his Humour ", and by sheer self-assertion forced his age to recognise him. It is far easier, therefore, to picture " rare Ben Jonson " than " myriad-minded Shakespeare ". But this very difficulty has induced those who love the works of the latter poet to attempt a re-creation of their creator, and in his own field of art, to re-vivify our national genius.

The life of Shakespeare has been taken as dramatic material by three present-day writers. Mr H. F. Rubinstein and Mr Clifford Bax, working together, have produced a play of which Mr A. W. Pollard says in his introduction " They have thought out their problem, their insoluble problem, and they present their view of it not argumentatively as a theory, but creatively in the five acts of a play ". This view, founded on the belief that Shakespeare was a disappointed and a disillusioned man (an estimate somewhat confirmed by a consideration of the " Sonnets ") is developed with constructive skill and is in keeping with the spirit of the sixteenth century. The " Will Shakespeare " of Miss Clemence Dane, on the other hand, is less probable but more romantic ; and is certainly " an invention " of beauty and passion. The difference in handling is no less marked in form than in thought ; the first-mentioned play is in prose, the latter in verse ; the former is Elizabethan, the second is Pre-Raphaelite. By the choice of prose the authors of " Shakespeare " have succeeded in conveying a feeling of reality, and the writer of the " Prefatory Note " can contend with justice that " If the first ' episode ' may be accepted as truly showing what Shakespeare was like in his early days as a playwright, the other episodes may be accepted ". This sense of reality is absent from the finely-modulated verse of " Will Shakespeare ". A comparison of various scenes from the two plays will make this evident.

The drama of joint authorship opens in the " First Episode ", dated 1592, with the business room of Philip Henslowe, and introduces us to " Kit " Marlowe, and later to Alleyne and Shakespeare. A clever touch is shown in the willingness of the " pawnbroker and theatrical adventurer " to pay a poor man ten crowns for properties while refusing them to Marlowe for a play. The dialogue which follows between the rival lovers, Alleyne and Shakespeare, over Joan Henslowe, is not only full of cleverly contrasted characteristics, but of considerable wit, and the several addresses of " Will " to Henslowe's daughter are full of the court conventions of the poet's early work, the Sonnet which he reads being from his first play, " Love's Labour's Lost ". The curse of Joan when she learns that Shakespeare is already married is both powerful and prophetic :—

" I pray heaven that you shall lose your heart to a woman without mercy, without scruple, without the least particle of kindness—no mortal, but a she-devil with beauty so ravishing that you shall count the sun black if she be not by you, and of spirit cold as a statue that you may dash yourself vainly against her contempt. I pray that she may draw you through all the torments of hell till you be utterly abased, till your insolence and your vanity be brought to the ground and you remember with misery the days when you looked upon life as a skittles-alley and the hearts of good maids as ninepins ! "

having the same spirit as the curse of Anne in the
first act of Miss Clemence Dane's drama, to which
we may now turn. The opening scene is very pain-
ful, and the colloquy of Shakespeare with his wife
very bitter, a bitterness emphasised by the beauty of
the verse and the images employed. The time is
earlier in the poet's career than in the former work,
and the point at issue is the departure of Shakespeare
to London. The scene must be read as a whole to
gain a full realisation of the passion and suffering of
Anne and the strange hardness of her husband.
Before her denunciation of the poet, Anne pleads
her cause in these lovely lines whose long metre is a
contrast to the surrounding pentameters :—

         " What gain but you?
The sight of your face and the sound of your foot on the
    stair,
And your casual word to a stranger—" This is my wife !"
For the touch of my hand on your arm, as a right, when
    we walked with the neighbours ;
For the son, for the son on my heart, with your smile
    and your frown :
For the loss of my name in the name that you gave when
    you said to him " Mother ! your mother ! "
For your glance at me over his head when he brought
    us his toys or his tears : . . ."

but Shakespeare replies, " Words ! Words ! You
lied to me. Go your own road ! I know you not ",
to be met with :—

        " But I, but I know you.
Have I not learned my god's face? Have I not seen
The great dreams cloud it, as the ships of the sky
Darken the river? . . ."

> " You're to be great, God pity you !
> I'm your poor village woman ; but I know
> What you must learn and learn, and shriek to God
> To spare you learning, if you will be great,
> Singing to men and women across fields
> Of years, and hearing answer as they reap,
> Afar, the centuried fields, ' He knew, He knew ! ' "

. . . .

> " How will they listen ? What ? I lied ? Oh, blind !
> When I, your own, show you my heart of hearts,
> A book for you to read all women by,
> Blindly you turn my page with—' Here are lies ' ! "

Still, however, the poet holds to his purpose to join
the players under Henslowe and seek " London ! The
future in a golden fog ! " while Anne sinks down by
the hearth with a cry of despair :—

> " But let me not again be cursed a woman
> Surrendered to the mercy of her man."

answered by the song of the approaching actors,
" Come with us to London ". Presently, when
Shakespeare is gone to prepare for his journey, the
players stream into the darkened room, Anne
unwillingly giving them welcome. At this point
occurs perhaps the most imaginative scene in the
play. As it were a pageant the actors foreshadow
the dramas of the poet. The pathetic dialogue
between Anne and the child of the company introduces a procession of Spirits who demand toll from
the shade of Shakespeare, " Tell our story ". The
authoress, with great skill, summarises a play in a
line given to a named spectre, as, for example, " A
Moor " " Dead lips, dead lips ! "—" A Crowned
Shadow " " He killed me while I slept "—" A Girl

19

dressed as a Boy " " I lived in a wood and laughed. Sing you my laughter when the sun shone ! " or by a single word—" A Man " (with a wand), " Dreams ! ", " The King in Rags ", " Frenzy ! ", " A Nun ", " Sacrament ! ", " A Drunkard ", " A Jest ! ". This is followed by the vision of three masked Fates which appear to Anne, she asks the second, " Who are you ? "

The SECOND MASK. " Fate ! his fate ! "

(*Dropping her veil she shows the face of a dark lady.*)

ANNE. " I knew, I knew ! Barren the ground beneath,
        No flowers, no fruit, spent arrows— "

(*The Second Mask makes way for the Third*). " Not the shears ! "

THIRD MASK (*Winding the thread*). " Not yet ! "

ANNE. " Who are you ? "

THIRD MASK.   " Fate ! his fate ! "

ANNE.   " A crown !

        My snake should know its fellow—is it so ? "

(*The mask is lifted and reveals the face of Elizabeth.*)

ANNE. I do not fear the Queen—

THIRD MASK.   Take back the thread !

(*She gives the distaff to the First Mask, who has re-appeared beside her, and glides away.*)

ANNE. But you I fear, O shrinking fate ! What fate? What first and last fate? Show me your face, I say !

(*She tears off the mask. The face revealed is the face of Anne. She screams.*) **Myself ! I saw myself ! Will ! Will !** (*The Child kneeling at the hearth stirs the fire and a bright flame shoots up that lights the whole room. It is empty save for the few players gathering together their bundles and Shakespeare who has hurried to Anne. His hand, gripping her shoulder, steadies her as she sways.*)

SHAKESPEARE. **Still railing?**

20

CHILD (*to his father*). She's a poor frightened lady and she cried. I like her.

ANNE. Gone! Gone! Where are they? Call them back! I saw—

SHAKESPEARE. What folly! These are players and my friends; you could have given them food at least and served them.

No apology need be made for quoting this scene at such length as it shows most clearly the difference in the handling of the subject in " Will Shakespeare " and " Shakespeare ". The use of the supernatural and the emotional stress which fill the former drama are absent from the latter, and yet, as will be seen later, the prose play has real pathos. Before returning to consider the " Second Episode " of it, the final speeches of Anne to Shakespeare must be quoted, if only in part, as a proof of the power of Miss Clemence Dane's verse and of its tragic quality :—

ANNE.   . . . Husband, when harvest comes,
        Of all your men and women I alone
        Can give you comfort, for you'll reap my pain
        As I your loss. What other knows our need?
        Dear hands, remember, when you hold her, thus,
        Close, close—

SHAKESPEARE.   Let go my hands!

ANNE.   and when she turns
        To stone, to a stone, to an unvouchsafing stone
        Under your clutch—

SHAKESPEARE.   You rave!

ANNE.   —loved hands, remember
        Me unloved then, and how my hands held you!
        And when her face—for I am prophecy—
        When her lost face, the woman I am not,
        Stares from the page you toil upon, thus, thus,

In a glass of tears, remember then that thus,
No other way,
I see your face between my work and me,
Always!

SHAKESPEARE.   Make end and let me go!

ANNE.   Why, go!
But mock me not with any " Let me go! "
I do not hold you. Ah, but when you're old
(You will be old one day, as I am old
Already in my heart), too weary-old
For love, hate, pity, anything but peace . . .
Come back to me—

SHAKESPEARE (*at the door*). Farewell!

ANNE.   —when all your need
Is hands to serve you and a breast to die on,
Come back to me—

SHAKESPEARE. Never in any world! (*He goes*).

ANNE (*crying out suddenly*). The years—the years
before me!

MRS HATHAWAY (*calling*). Anne! Anne! Where are
you? Why, what do you here, in the cold, in the dark,
and all alone?

ANNE. I wait.

After the emotion of this scene it is quieting to
turn to the " Second Episode " of " Shakespeare ",
dated 1596. The poet is found in his lodging in St.
Helen's Bishopsgate, at work on " Romeo and
Juliet ", refusing to join Heminges, the actor, in his
walk in the fields. Presently the " Dark Lady "
enters seeking, as she says, rest from the babbling
tongues below. The love scene between them which
follows is written with restraint and naturalness, but
has many shrewd touches, as, for instance, when
" Rosaline " says to Shakespeare of Anne :—

" You loved her, Will. Before you had her, you loved
—but a passion that's dead has the sickly smell of dead

lilies and we say to ourselves—' That? *That* was not love ! ' "

where her image is borrowed from the couplet :—

> " For sweetest things turn sourest by their deeds
> Lilies that fester smell far worse than weeds."

and when he answers her about his marriage, the tragedy is summed up in the simple words :—

" Not to her, Rosaline, did I lose my heart, but to the merry clouds of spring that were above her and the green rye through which I saw her coming. Our families did the rest—cooped up in a parlour for hours on end, while all the summer squandered itself outside, and prating of honour and the girl's innocence. Dead lilies— fling them away ! "

The conversation then turns upon Shakespeare's son, Hamnet, of whom the poet talks with enthusiasm, even though Rosaline points out that the child is one who is " doated upon so extremely that for ten years you have never journeyed to see him ! " The " Dark Lady " then expresses her longing to act a player's part, and when the poet doubts her capacity to do so she says :—

" A certain lord whom in these parts we call Proteus, has declared that could I but present a subtle woman, a woman of your devising, I should make all London dizzy ".

Soon Mr " W. H.", the Proteus, enters, and in course of his talk quotes the Ballade of Villon, " Des Femmes de Paris ". After some words he and Rosaline go out and leave the poet at work; but a few moments later " Proteus " returns and tells Shakespeare that a poor woman from Stratford is seeking him and is waiting below. This dialogue follows :—

WILL. I thank you. 'Tis Anne—my wife.

W. H. As I feared. Shall I give her direction to some honest tavern?

WILL. She has footed from Stratford, you say . . . And at least she could give me news of Hamnet. She is alone? I pray you, bid her come in.

The " Dark Lady " then enters disguised as Anne, and in the conversation that ensues tells the poet that " his soul is indeed damned and without repentance " and that Hamnet " if the Lord see good, will grow into a notable preacher ".

WILL. Is it so that you babble to the boy? Nay, I've a mind to go to Stratford . . .

" ANNE ". Will!

WILL. If it be but to show him the Bible of the earth and to teach him to quire with the birds! Yet I cannot come. I am fast in London.

" Anne " then tells him that until he is washed clean he shall never return to Stratford, to which the poet replies :

" To-morrow, Anne, I shall fare to Stratford, and I shall rest in the village for a matter of two weeks. Thereafter I shall return hither—with Hamnet! "

The next instant Mr " W. H." again enters and the deception is revealed, Rosaline saying, " Who was it doubted my skill? Who swore never to give me lodgment here? And who was it said he would never go back to Stratford? ", and Shakespeare answering, " And have I gone back to Stratford? " (laughing heartily) " by my soul 'twas well done—the blackest of nightmares but the blithest of jests! " At this moment Will Kemp. and two players burst in and say that " young Morley " has found an air for Will's

24

song. The " Dark Lady " demands that it should be sung and Shakespeare fetches his lute. Just, however, as they are preparing to listen, tragedy enters. John Heminges arrives unceremoniously and gives a letter to Shakespeare, who reads it, the rest remaining silent.

W. H. My friend ! Ill news?
WILL. Hamnet—he's dead.
DARK LADY (*Running forward in tears*). Will !
W. H. (*Also going to him*). What can I do?
WILL (*Dazed and moving away from them*). I must go—to Stratford—to-night.
W. H. I'll help you put up your chattels, Will.
(*Shakespeare and Mr W. H. set about preparing necessities for the journey.*)
DARK LADY (*seemingly heartless*). Kemp—the music.
KEMP (*shocked*). What, Lady?
DARK LADY (*imperiously*). Sing it—

As Kemp finishes the lyric " Come away, come away, death ", Shakespeare hurries out. There is nothing indeed in this " Episode " which seems out of keeping with the time, and the only point for doubt is whether the poet would have been deceived by Rosaline's disguise. The dialogue is flowing, and the introduction of the tragic note and the song from " Twelfth Night " finely handled.

But it is time to turn once more to the passionate drama of Miss Clemence Dane. The Second Act is in two scenes. The first reveals Elizabeth in a room of the Palace discussing with Henslowe the respective merits of Marlowe and Shakespeare. The conversation is in prose. Henslowe says of the latter poet :—

" With his laughter he locks the door of his heart against every man ".
ELIZABETH. And every woman?

HENSLOWE. They say—no, Madam!

ELIZABETH. Then we must find her.

HENSLOWE (*with a glance at Mary Fitton, who has been in the background at the virginal*). They say she is found already. But a court lady—and a player!

Elizabeth then calls Mary to her and asks her whether Shakespeare or Marlowe is the coming man. Mary favours the second. The Queen then says of the former, " I forget if ever I saw him ", and Henslowe breaks out into this fine description of Shakespeare:

" Madam, if ever you saw him, you would not forget—
A small, a proud head, like an Arab Christ,
And noble, madman's fingers, never still—
The face still though, mouth hid, the nostril wide,
And eyes like voices calling, shrill and sad,
Borne on hot winds from fairyland or hell;
Yet round the heavy lids a score of lines
All criss-cross crinkle like a score of laughs
That he has scribbled hastily down himself
With his quick fingers . . ."

Elizabeth then asks Henslowe to bring Shakespeare, and says she will see Marlowe another time.

HENSLOWE. I'll fetch him to you. (*Henslowe goes out*).

ELIZABETH. To you, Mary—to you!

MARY. O Madam, spare me! It's a stiff instrument and once, I think, has been ill-tuned.

ELIZABETH. Tune it afresh!

MARY. You wish that, Madam?

ELIZABETH. I wish it. Marlowe can wait—and Pembroke.

In this harsh way the Queen orders Mary to attract Shakespeare, probably with the idea of adding to her own glory, and after a few more words goes out.

The next moment Shakespeare enters. The dialogue which follows passes from witty repartee to a fine description by the poet of his own mind, " My mind's not one room stored, but many . . .", and then to a more serious note when the dramatist says that he will show her " Fairyland, and you and me in it ". Mary replies, " Give me flesh and blood, not gossamer,

> " Honey and heart-ache, and a lovers' moon ".
> SHAKESPEARE. I read of lovers once in Italy—
>   She was like you, such eyes of night, such hair.
>   God took a week to make his world, but these
>   In four short days made heaven to burn on earth
>   Like a great torch; and when they died—
> MARY. They died
> SHAKESPEARE. Like torches quenched in water,
>   suddenly,
>   Because they loved too well.
>
>   .   .   .   .
>
> MARY. What shall we call it, Will?
>   The Tragical Discourse? The Famous End?
>   The Lovers of Verona?
> SHAKESPEARE.   No, no! Plain.
>   Their two names married—Romeo and Juliet.

This scene lacks the simplicity and directness of that between " Will " and the " Dark Lady " in the other drama under consideration. The attitude of Elizabeth, however, is not unlike our conception of her character, and we sympathise with Mary. It is, however, doubtful whether Shakespeare would have allowed himself to be drawn into a trap so easily. While it may be said that the whole scene is imaginary rather than real this should not blind us to the fineness of the verse nor the emotional handling of the persons. We are left indeed with the following conclusion. In the " Shakespeare " the scene is allowed to mould the characters; in the drama of Miss Clemence Dane, the characters the scene.

The next scene in " Will Shakespeare " brings us into the theatre on the first night of " Romeo and Juliet ", and is full of dramatic motion and colour. It opens with the excitement at the success of the play and a fine apostrophe by Shakespeare to his achievement, made more wonderful for him by Mary's appreciation (under the favour of the Queen) to whom he attributes the drama. But this joyous moment is followed by sadness. Mrs Hathaway appears with the tragic news of the illness of the poet's son, and in the bitter words of his mother-in-law, the poet begins to feel remorse and breaks out into a magnificent reply to her affirmation.

" Sixty years I have learned lessons in the world; but I never learned that a city was better than green fields, friends better than a house-mate, or the works of a man's hand more to him than the child of his own flesh ".

beginning :

" And have I learned it, I ? Do I not know
That when I left her I left all behind
That was my right ? See how I live my life—
Married nor single, neither bond nor free,
My future mortgaged for a roofless home ! . . ."

which is intercepted by the subtle description of Anne's agony, of his child's illness, and of his dying cries for his " Father ". Shakespeare suddenly realises all this, and says " I will come ", promising to be on London Bridge at midnight. Mrs Hathaway goes and Mary enters saying that the Queen is waiting for him; when he is gone Mary and Marlowe, who is standing by, meet and a dialogue ensues. Suddenly

Henslowe comes in to say that the boy who is playing Juliet has fallen and hurt his arm, and that the
play will be ruined. Mary says she will play the part
and while she does so Marlowe and the poet talk, the
latter telling his friend his sorrow and asking :

> " Oh, is there peace
> Anywhere, Kit, in any, any world? "

begs him to tell the house that he is gone away.
Marlowe although amazed at the poet throwing away
his fortune promises and goes out to do so. Shakespeare is also preparing to depart when Mary enters
in her Juliet robes and breaks forth exultantly :—

> " Oh, I faced
> The peacock of the world, the arch of eyes
> That watched me love a god, the eyes, eyes, eyes,
> That watched me die of love. Wake me again,
> O soul that did inhabit me, O husband
> Whose mind I uttered, to whose will I swayed,
> Whose self of love I was ! Wake me again
> To die of love in earnest ! "

The passion of this and of her next outburst com-
mencing "I cannot ride this hurricane" sweep
over the poet and in the lines

> " These are the hands I never held till now ;
> These are the lips I never felt on mine ;
> This is the hour I dreamed of, many an hour ;
> This is the spirit awake. God in your sky,
> Did your heart beat so on the seventh dawn ? "

surrenders himself to her love, but is suddenly
wakened from his ecstasy by a voice :—

> SHAKESPEARE. In my heart I heard it cry
> Like a sick child waked suddenly at night
> (*Cyring out*) A child—a sick child ! Unlink your arms
> that hold me !

MARY. Never till I choose!
SHAKESPEARE. Put back your hair! I am lost
　Unless I lose all gain. O moonless night,
　In your hot darkness I have lost my way!
　But kiss me, summer, once! On London Bridge
　At midnight—I'll be there! Has the clock struck?
MARY. Midnight long since.
SHAKESPEARE. Oh, I am damned and lost
　　　In hell for ever!

Mary asks him if damnation is not sweet, and then glorifies their passion in wonderful verse, the poet cries:

　　　　　　　　　　　　　　　　Eve,
Eve, Eve, the snake has been with you! You draw,
You drink my soul as I your body—
MARY.　　　　　　　　　　　　　　　Kiss!

It is difficult to criticise this scene as one is carried away by the emotion and the poetry, but the impression left on the mind is one of gorgeous colour rather than clear drawing. The verse also, though most musical and balanced, lacks the power of restraint, and the remark of Courthope in his " Life in Poetry, Law in Taste " may perhaps be applied to it: " In criticising the language of a modern poet, look in his verse to see if it possesses the hereditary national quality of condensing thought in an epigrammatic form ". Powerful as is " Will Shakespeare " it appears to lack this merit of condensation both in form and in thought.

The scene of the " Third Episode " of " Shakespeare " is also laid in a theatre. It is the " Globe " at a rehearsal of " Hamlet ", and is dated 1602. We are introduced to Shakespeare and Mr W. H. discussing the merits of the play. The latter is trying to cheer the poet with praises of his work, but he rails bitterly at the wantonness of fame. Presently the "Dark Lady" enters, and describes how exacting her mistress has become, but even she cannot cheer Shakespeare who, in reply to her remark that if he would take his losses more stoically he would find her and Mr W. H. honest friends, says:

"Honest, you say—honest? You were wiser to remain as you are, for I warn you that in this world an honest mind is every villain's football. Did I not love you, I could rail at your perfidy, but that's where I stick and that was the cause of my undoing. I loved you well, Proteus, and you stole her away by night".

The "Dark Lady" is about to take her leave when Burbage comes in and talks of Robinson, the Queen in Hamlet, the poet expressing his anger at the vanity of the boy. He is about to present the "Grave Scene" when the dramatist springs up crying, "Stay, stay! We will have the 'Closet Scene'." The actor demurs, saying that it had been well played the day before, but is overruled, the poet saying, "Burbage—your rapier! I'll show you how to play Hamlet".

BURBAGE. Come, Will, you have laurels enough. You are a great poet, man. In the playing, content yourself with my poor skill.
WILL. For once I'll be actor, too!
W. H. Well, even Homer nodded.
KEMP. True, sir—but he never snored.
WILL. Your rapier—for the Closet Scene.
W. H. Best humour him, Master Burbage!

Shakespeare then proceeds to act with the greatest excitement the interview between Hamlet and his Mother, watching all the time its effect on "Rosa-

line ". In his passion he adds and alters the passages
as, for instance :

> " Look here, upon this picture, and on this,
> The counterfeit presentment of two "—friends.

Break not in upon me—I care not for the words. The
counterfeit presentment of two friends whereof was one
that loved thee so well, so profoundly, that with his love
in thy heart thou mightest have plumbed all mysteries ;
but him hast thou spurned away to follow that other—
a painted image, a gilded mockery, a lovely and hollow
eidolon, whose heart is a nest for the viper-brood of
treachery ! "

and when Robinson, as the Queen, says, " Thou
turnst mine eyes into my very soul ", he mutters
" Is it so indeed ? " Presently " The Dark Lady's
head falls back against a supporting wall " and the
poet cries, " Ah, God ! I have done too well ! " Burbage, " She has swooned ? "

DARK LADY (*opening her eyes*). Swooned ? Not I,
Master Burbage. 'Twas my drowsiness overcame me.

WILL. What—you slept ?

DARK LADY. Your ranting, Will, was so tedious . . .

WILL. Kemp—I have failed to entertain this lady.
I shall not try again. I have tried too long. Do you
present the ditty of which we have heard such tales—
and so make our amends.

Kemp then sings " In youth, when I did love, did
love . . .", and Shakespeare goes to the corner of
the stage and when laughter breaks out snaps the
rapier across his knee.

This act is dramatic, but in an entirely different
way from the theatre scene in " Will Shakespeare ".
It shows the writers' gifts of causing a comparatively
simple incident to become of interest by its treatment, and the use of the famous scene by Shakespeare

as his method of condemning " Rosaline " is in keeping with the character of the poet presented in this
drama, as is his symbolic breaking of the rapier.
While it has far less emotional passion than the
situation of Miss Clemence Dane's presentment, it
has more reality and spontaneity. So far it has been
possible to consider scenes in the two dramas under
discussion which bear a resemblance to each other.
The quarrel of Joan and Will, and her curse upon
him has been compared with that between Shakespeare and Anne and the latter's denunciation; the
love scene between Will and Rosaline, with that
between Mary and Shakespeare; and, lastly, the first
performance of " Romeo and Juliet " with the
rehearsal of " Hamlet ". After this, however, the
plays diverge, that by the joint authors following
out their conception of the poet as a disappointed
and disillusioned man; that of the single writer working up to the Queen's insistence on Shakespeare
working, whatever it may cost him, for the sake of
England, haunted by the bitter memories of the
past.

The first scene of the third act of Miss Dane's
drama is set in Shakespeare's lodging, where he and
Marlowe are discussing their respective works. After
a few moments the conversation turns on " Mary ",
the former lamenting that he has not seen her for
some time, and the latter affirming " that she never
liked him better ". Shakespeare then asks Kit if
he blames him for remaining in London, and
Marlowe says :

" For this prize, if I loved her, I would pay away all
I had.

SHAKESPEARE. Honour, Kit?
MARLOWE. Honour, Will !

SHAKESPEARE. Faith and conscience and an only son?

MARLOWE. It's my own life. What are children to me?

SHAKESPEARE. Well, I have paid ".

The elder dramatist then tells his friend that he is maddened by worry, and hearing a step on the stairs thinks it must be that of the boy he had sent to Mary; but it is Henslowe, who, after " pounding at the door ", enters and speaks sharply to Marlowe, who replies, " You see, they'll make rivals of us, Will, before they've done ", and then goes out to journey to Deptford. Henslowe then recounts to Shakespeare the tour his company has made, and when he mentions that they had acted at Stratford, the poet asks whether he saw Anne. Then follows a delicate if pathetic piece of writing, in which the actor describes to the dramatist his call at his house. He touches on the beauty of the garden, and says:

HENSLOWE. " I spoke of you. She listened.
SHAKESPEARE. Questioned you?
HENSLOWE. Never a question.
SHAKESPEARE. She said nothing?
HENSLOWE. Nothing.
SHAKESPEARE. Not like her.
HENSLOWE. But her eyes spoke . . .
. . . so, as I turned to go
I asked her—" Any greeting? " Then she said,
Lifting her chin as if she sped her words
Far, far, like pigeons flung upon the air,
And soft her voice as bird-wings—then she said,
" Tell him the woods are green at Shottery,
Fuller of flowers than any wood in the world ".
" What else? " said I. She said—" The wind still blows
Fresh between park and river. Tell him that ! "

Said I, " No message, letter ? " Then she said,
Twisting her hands—" Tell him the days are long.
Tell him— " and suddenly ceased ".

Henslowe then argues with Shakespeare his remiss-
ness in not having prepared the new play that they
had promised, and the poet replies with bitterness,
" I'm to live, not write. Tell that to the Queen ".
At this moment the boy enters and says that there is
no answer, although unobserved he saw Mary.
Henslowe tells Shakespeare that Marlowe has usurped
his place in her affections, and as a proof asks the
boy to sing the popular ditty he was humming as he
came, of which two lines were :—

" Turn about and turn about,
Kit pops in as Will pops out ! "

Shakespeare then learns from the boy that " Mary"
in man's disguise, has set out for Deptford, and
furious, throws a purse to his messenger and rushes
out ; leaving Henslowe determined to take the matter
to the Queen.

The second scene in this act brings us into the inn-
parlour at Deptford, where Marlowe is drinking with
his companions. The landlord tells him that a young
man is without who wants to see him. The poet is
for sending the guest away but, on the persuasion of
his host, sends him to bring the traveller in. Marlowe is astounded, and takes Mary into another room,
rebuking her rashness. She, however, addresses
Marlowe passionately, and he tells her that Shakespeare is married although he has not seen his wife
for ten years. Mary is furious, and throws herself
into the arms of the poet, who forgets his friendship
and loyalty to Shakespeare in the ecstasy of the

moment. Suddenly Shakespeare enters quietly by the window, having overheard :—

MARLOWE. " Let's have no more ! You know
          I loved—I love the man.
MARY.   Why, so do I.
MARLOWE. You shall not !
MARY. Then I will not. Not to-night.
SHAKESPEARE. Why not to-night, my lover and my
          friend ?
      Will you not give me wine and welcome me ?
      Sit down, sit down—we three have much to say !

      .   .   .   .

      Part ! Part, I say ! Part ! lest I couple you
      Once and for all !
MARY. He's armed !
MARLOWE.   He shall not touch you ! . . .
(*Marlowe darts at Shakespeare and is thrown off. He staggers against the table, knocking over the candle. As he strikes the second time his arm is knocked up, striking his own forehead. He falls across the bed. There is an instant's pause, then Shakespeare rushes to him, slipping an arm under his shoulder.*)
MARY. Dead ? Is he dead ? Oh, what an end !
      I never saw a dead man. Will—to me !
SHAKESPEARE. Get help !
MARY.   I dare not.
MARLOWE.   Oh !
SHAKESPEARE. What is it ?
MARLOWE.   Oh !
      My life, my lovely life, and cast away
      Untasted, wasted—
      Death, let me go ! (*He dies.*) "

Shakespeare breaks out into eulogies of the dead poet, and then forces from Mary the admission that she never loved him. During this passionate dialogue

the dramatist hears the voice of Anne—" At Shottery
the woods are green ". Finally Mary flies, leaving
Shakespeare alone, and a little later Henslowe enters,
saying the Queen wants him. Henslowe manages to
convince the landlord and the drinkers that Marlowe
is dead drunk, getting his friend away with difficulty,
while the crowd hammer on the table singing :—

> " Ho, boy ! Hey, boy !
> Come this way, boy !
> Who'll have a drink with me ?
> Hey, Death ! Ho, Death !
> Out you go, Death !
> We'll never drink with thee ! "

*(The door swings to and quiet settles on the lighten-
ing room. The first ray of sunlight touches the bed.
Outside the birds are beginning to sing.)*

Both this and the previous scene are full of beautiful poetry, but are dramatically too profuse. In the
first Henslowe's description of his visit to Stratford,
and in the second the long eulogies of Shakespeare
on Marlowe, do not help forward the action. In the
former case the poet would probably have been in
too great impatience to listen to his friend's account,
and in the second it is unlikely that after a tavern
death, the two actors in the tragedy would speak at
such length. In this act the authoress has sacrificed
reality of event to poetic opportunity. The whole
series of incidents in the play is, from what we know,
improbable ; and in this act it is more evident than
formerly, for it is less restrained and subordinated
to the main theme of the drama. The quarrel
between Shakespeare and Marlowe over Mary and the
latter's death are rather forced situations, and the
passion of the scenes is not so dramatically simple as

the symbolic breaking of the rapier by the poet in " Shakespeare ".

To this play we may now return. The " Fourth Episode " is dated 1608, and opens in the parlour of Montjoy, a wig-maker of Cheapside, where Shakespeare has lodgings. At the commencement, Madame Montjoy and Burbage are discussing a wig, but presently the talk slips to the poet who is melancholy and disillusioned. Burbage says, " That Will should be failing now—at two-score years and four, when his power should ride the meridian ", and then mentions Ben Jonson and his attitude to his fellow-dramatists. Presently Shakespeare enters, and in reply to the actor's remarks is very bitter, saying, among other satirical remarks, " I see through you all. You loved me for what you might get of me ". This hurts Burbage who leaves with wishes for his recovery. Madame Montjoy then tells the poet of her visit to Mistress Milton (this is a clever touch as the poet was born in December, 1608) and describes how she looked into the " Mermaid " seeing—

" Masters Fletcher and Rowley and Marston and Webster and—oh, yes, Master Ford alone in a corner ".

but not Ben Jonson. Shakespeare then breaks out into a tirade against the latter. Madame, in distress to see the poet so bitter and satirical, suggests some music to cheer him, but he demands paper on which to write. He frightens her by his remark, " To-night I think I *shall* sleep " and goes out. At this moment Jonson enters, with some stealth, and the terrified woman tells him of her fears. He gruffly but kindly comforts her, and when she says that perhaps the sight of his daughter Judith might cheer the poet, says that he has already brought her to town, full of fear at being carried away from Stratford. They arrange that she shall come to Cheapside. He goes out, and Shakespeare enters and reads—

" The last will and testament of me, Thersites Modernus, alias Timon of Cheapside, alias William Shakespeare of Stratford-on-Avon. . . . And, lastly, to the Evil Spirit who devised the world of men I leave my malediction and therewith, like Job aforetime, I do curse the day that I was born and do give my soul, together with my body, most willingly to the worms ".

The poet, while waiting for a taper with which to seal this bitter document, sinks despairingly into a chair; and a moment later Madame Montjoy ushers in Judith who, frightened, remains close to the door. Shakespeare sees her but at first does not recognise his daughter. He says, " Who are you, child? " (No answer) " What would you here? " (No answer. Shakespeare rises and goes over to her) " What! Is it possible? Judith? "

JUDITH (*looking up*). Father, father! Then the rough man spoke truth! (*She runs into his arms.*)
WILL. Dear heart—how came you? Who was it worked this wonder?
JUDITH. A dreadful huge fellow . . .

The poet realises that this must be Jonson, and after Judith has described how she will comfort and cheer him at Stratford, " The meadows there are covered with cowslips, and the oaks are beginning to leaf. And in the copses there are primroses and violets—hundreds and hundreds "; released from a prolonged strain, breaks down, Judith crying, " Father—my dear !" In an upper room the daughter of Madame Montjoy begins to sing, " Hark! hark! the lark at heaven's gate sings ".

JUDITH. Take me to Stratford! You will?
WILL. Ah, Judith—*you* shall take *me* ".

And, as the song continues, Shakespeare tears into fragments " the last will of Thersites Modernus ", and the scene closes.

This " Episode " is remarkable for its realism, and is full of clever touches; Madame Montjoy's reference to Mistress Milton and the " Mermaid "; the character of Ben is subtly suggested in his kindness of heart and roughness of method; the bitterness of the poet is compressed in the sarcasm and irony of the " Will " and the tenderness of Judith delicately defined by her words. It is the more pathetic as a scene because it is so simply expressed, yet it is filled with careful art. It proves once more that in " Will Shakespeare " the characters live in a world of emotional colour, but in " Shakespeare " the surroundings are those of real life. To combine probable accuracy of fact with affecting presentation is no small achievement, and this " Episode " is very fine in its dramatic restraint and balance.

The final act of Miss Clemence Dane's " Invention " is difficult to criticise. The events may be given simply. Elizabeth is found in a room of the Palace overlooking the street, and when her maid-of-honour says :

" I wonder, Madam, that you choose this room
  Here on the noisy street—
ELIZABETH. Child, when you marry
  Who'll rule your nursery, you or your maids?
GIRL. Why, that I will!
ELIZABETH. Then you must sit in it daily ".

She then asks, " Where's Mary Fitton? " and the maid-of-honour answers that she is in waiting but half asleep, having been up early to pick roses, as the Queen bade her. Elizabeth replies " As I bade her ? " and then tells the girl to open the window so that she may hear the cry of a passing hawker, and to fetch her purse. While she is gone Elizabeth takes out her purse from a drawer and throws money to the woman, who sings':—

> " I plucked my riches
> From Deptford ditches,
> I came by a Deptford Inn;
> Where a young man lies,
> With pennies on his eyes—
>   Murdered, lady, and none saw who did it !
> Cress ! buy cress ! "

The girl returns and when she is distressed at being unable to find the purse the Queen says " It was here ", and tells her to ask the seller whence she comes, and when the answer is " From Marlow ", says " Marlow's across the river, far from us ", to which Elizabeth answers, "Marlowe's across the river, far from us ". The Queen then discovers that Mary has forgotten her duty and not informed her of the arrival of Henslowe and Shakespeare, and tells the girl to send Henslowe, and, when she rings, Mary. Henslowe enters and is surprised to find that Elizabeth already knows of Marlowe's death, and she replies in a magnificent speech ending :—

> " I know what darkness does, what dawn discovers
> In all the English country. I am the Queen ".

He tells her that Shakespeare is in a dazed condition, but that he does not believe him to have been the murderer. Elizabeth says, " Well, I'll see Shakespeare ", and rings for Mary, who enters. The Queen then bids her tell him to " hurry ", which she

does and the voice is recognised by Henslowe, who
goes out; Mary is about to fetch Shakespeare when
Elizabeth checks her and asks her " Why are you
not in black, Mary ? " " I, Madam ? " " Marlowe
is dead ". The Queen then traps her into revealing
herself.

" You Mary Fitton ! For by your dark-ringed eyes
　Your dreaming service and those blind hands of yours
　Seeking a hold, I think you saw him die,
　Ere you passed Henslowe in the dark, crying
　　' Hurry ! ' "

Mary retorts that it was the Queen's errand, and a
passionate scene ensues, the Queen questioning the
woman, and she growing more and more angry.
Finally, Elizabeth saying that Mary shall be banished
to the country, she asks " Upon what count ? "

ELIZABETH.　　　　On none. But I've no time
　No room for butter-fingers. Here's a man slain
　Upon your lap that England needed. Go !
　Go, blunted tool ! (She touches a bell.)
MARY. Madam ! Madam ! You wrong me !
ELIZABETH. I've wronged your betters, Mary, Mary
　　Fitton,
　As tide wrongs pebble, or as wind wrongs chaff
　At threshing time.

Mary demands justice from the Queen of England,
but Elizabeth holds to her purpose and as she goes
and meets Shakespeare as he enters with the words—
　　　　　　You come to cue !
SHAKESPEARE. What has fallen ?
MARY.　　　　　Sent away
　Because of you, because my name is Mary !
SHAKESPEARE. Go to my lodging ! Wait for me ! I'll
　　follow
　For where you go I go.

MARY. Ay, bring your wife!
This act is over! There are other men!
(She goes out.)
SHAKESPEARE. Mary! Love, life, the breath I breathe,
come back!
Mary, you have not heard me! Mary! Mary!
Come back! *(The door shuts with a clang.)*
ANNE'S Voice. Come back!
ELIZABETH. Never, in any world!
Fasten the door there!
SHAKESPEARE *(struggling to open it)*. Open! Open,
I say!

But in vain, and while he struggles Elizabeth mocks
him. When he is quieter the Queen demands from
him the play he promised, he cries out:

" I am to live, not write,
To love, not write of love, to live my life
As others do, to live a summer life
As all the others do! "

To this Elizabeth replies in a wonderful speech
beginning " I thought so too when I was young
. . . ", and ends " Yet, to-night I crown my heir.
I, England, crown my son ".

SHAKESPEARE. There was a better man but yesterday—
To him the crown! King was he of all song.
ELIZABETH. He's king now of the silence after
song . . ."

Later she says:

" Here is the bill—reckon it ere you pay!
SHAKESPEARE. Have I not paid?
ELIZABETH. Nay, hourly, till you die.
. . . .
These are your days. I tell you, I, a queen,
Ruling myself and half a world. I know
What fate is laid upon you. Carry it!

48

Or, if you choose, flinch, weaken, and fall down,
Lie flat and howl, and let the ones that love you
(Not burdened less) half carry it and you!
Will you do that? Proud man, will you do that?"
SHAKESPEARE. Because you are all woman—
ELIZABETH. Have you seen it?
None other sees.
SHAKESPEARE. —and not as you're the Queen,
I'll let you be the tongue to my own soul,
Yet not for long I'll bear it ".

Elizabeth then describes her own early love and
says to the poet:
" Bury it deep!
SHAKESPEARE. Deep as my sorrow lies.
But, Queen, what cometh after?
ELIZABETH. Work.
SHAKESPEARE. And after?
ELIZABETH. Sleep comes for me.
SHAKESPEARE. And after?
ELIZABETH. Sleep for you.
SHAKESPEARE. And after?
ELIZABETH. Nothing. Only the blessed sleep.
SHAKESPEARE. And so ends all?
ELIZABETH. And so all ends.
SHAKESPEARE. Love ends?
ELIZABETH. And so love ends ".

Shakespeare takes his pen to write, and Elizabeth
has the door flung open, the poet says bitterly,
" What do I here? . . . There's nothing left but
words ". As the Queen leaves him she says, " Is
the harness heavy—heavy? ", and he replies " Heavy
as lead. Heavy as a heart ". For the remainder of
this impressive scene the poet tries to write but is
haunted by the voice of Anne, and the vision of Mary.
He struggles against it, but finally, when he hears his
wife's words :—

44

> " I alone
> Can give you comfort, for you reap my pain,
> As I your loss—loss—loss—

SHAKESPEARE. Anne, was it thus?

ANNE'S Voice. No other way—

SHAKESPEARE. Such pain?

ANNE'S Voice. Such pain, such pain!

SHAKESPEARE. I did not know. O tortured thing,
remember!
I did not know—I did not know! Forgive—

ANNE'S Voice. Forgiving is forgetting—no, come
back!
I love you. Oh, come back to me, come back!

SHAKESPEARE. I cannot ".

He then breaks out into an impassioned questioning, " What is this love? " ending

> " I believe and know
> That the Pit's bottom is the lap of God
> And God is love.

ANNE'S Voice. Is love, is love—

SHAKESPEARE. I know.
And knowing I will live my dark days out
And wait for His own evening to give light ".

So he sets to work tortured my memories and
regrets, and the drama ends :—

SHAKESPEARE. " No comfort anywhere.

ANNE'S Voice. I love you so.

SHAKESPEARE. The work, the work remains.

ANNE'S Voice. But when you're old,
For work too old, or pity, love or hate,
For anything but peace, and in your hand
Lies the crowned life victorious at last—

SHAKESPEARE. Like the crowned Indian fruit, the
voyage home
Rots while it gilds, not worth the tasting—

ANNE'S Voice. Then,

45

> Remember me! Then, then, when all your need
> Is hands to serve you and a breast to die on,
> Come back to me!
>
> SHAKESPEARE.   God knows—some day?
> ANNE'S Voice.   I wait ".
>
> (*As he stoops over his work again.*) (*Curtain.*)

No apology is necessary for quoting this scene at such length as it is perhaps filled with finer poetry than any other in the play. The authoress shows great skill in linking it up with the first act by repeating phrases used by Anne, and by fulfilling her prophecy. While the interview between Shakespeare and Elizabeth is improbable, the action of the Queen with regard to Mary Fitton is not out of keeping with her historical character, and her speeches have the ring of true eloquence and poetry. As in the early acts of Miss Dane's " Invention " the atmosphere is one of passionate intensity, and while the conclusion of the play is effective, it lacks the note of peace which concludes the greatest works, for the impression left on the mind is one of strain and uncertainty. This is not so in the case of the prose play.

The " Fifth Episode " of " Shakespeare " has an atmosphere of repose. The scene is the living-room at " New Place ", Stratford, and the year 1616. Shakespeare and his solicitor, Collins, are discussing the former's will. The lawyer asks the dramatist if he has not some shares in the theatre in London, and he replies that they were sold the previous year. Their chat continues until Collins says, " We have now to deal only with—with the marriage portion for Mistress Judith ". Shakespeare answers, " We will put that question aside". The solicitor is not satisfied, and tries to settle the point, but the poet is firm. Presently Anne enters and with unwillingness asks the lawyer to stay and sup. He accepts and goes with the dramatist into the garden. When Shakespeare returns, and Collins is a moment absent, Anne says angrily that his obstinacy is breaking Judith's heart, but her father will not relent. Anne goes out and brings in a " Young Poet " who has ridden from London to see him, and then retires. The visitor addresses Shakespeare in flattering terms, touching on his own qualifications for appreciation, and begging him, for the sake of humanity, to take some thought for his manuscripts which might have all perished in the fire at the " Globe ". He offers to collect and edit, under the guidance of the poet, the plays which he knows so well—" I warrant you, sir, it would be a labour of love ". Shakespeare, however, replies, " Good friend, in every disinterested action there is beauty. I thank you for your zeal, but I must impress upon you that you urge me in vain ". The young man then sketches in a wonderful passage the life of the dramatist as revealed in his plays, and when he finishes :—

" And through all these varying pictures—may I not say it, sir?—I recognise the dignity and the pride of genius.

WILL. And after " The Tempest "?

POET. There is nothing after.

WILL. There is something which you do not know yet.

POET. What, sir?

WILL. The desire to forget it.

POET. To forget . . .? "

At this moment Judith enters, and the young poet exclaims, " A daughter of Shakespeare ! Where shall I find fit words? " But to this the dramatist replies :

" The simplest were the best, for she is no poet and can neither read nor write. (*The Young Poet recoils in astonishment.*) All my care I bestowed upon children of another kind—children who in these days bring me no consolation. Only she—returning good for evil—has been my stay in a time of darkness ".

Judith, sitting on a stool at her father's feet, tells him that her lover has fallen in with his wishes and written him a letter. Shakespeare gives this to the poet to read, and when he finds that the young man says, " Moreover, in conformity with your express desire, I promise that, if ever I go to London, I will not set foot in a playhouse . . .", he allows the paper to drop from his hand and sinks into a chair, the dramatist saying, " Well, sir, you have read your answer ", and then continuing :

" A little wisdom is worth a heavy price. Long since, not knowing the vanity of ambition, I gave my whole heart to my writings. You, in your generosity, would recall them to me, but, like the hopes and hazards of a fruitless voyage, I wish now to remember them no more ".

Judith's voice is heard from the garden, " Father —we have found some white violets ! "

WILL. Come, sir, you shall see my garden. In *that* I have some pride, for that is God's work. Ah, Master Collins ! (*He goes out and joins Collins, the Young Poet is about to follow him but, dropping into a chair, buries his face in his hands.*)

JUDITH (*standing at the open door, a little dismayed*). Young Master ! Is anything amiss? (*A brief pause.*)

POET (*looking up, and speaking in a broken voice*). You would not know the song.

JUDITH. What song, sir?

POET (*reciting the words softly and upon two or three notes*).

Full fathom five thy father lies . . .

(*He rises unsteadily, and passes with Judith into the garden.*) "

There is a wonderful sense of peace in this conclusion. The master-poet, disillusioned and disappointed, turns to forgetfulness, to his daughter and to Nature for rest. It is a daring solution to the mystery surrounding the last days of Shakespeare, but is quite justified from the point of view taken by the authors. One may agree with Mr A. W. Pollard that "A belief that Shakespeare from first to last was more truly master of his own soul than is here shown may be my own contribution to the 'idolatry' from which few lovers of his plays escape", but still admire the realistic and dramatic achievement of the authors.

The comparison of these two plays is now completed, and it only remains to summarise the conclusions and to attempt an estimate of their value as pictures of the poet and as literature. In the first case it must be mentioned that the authors of "Shakespeare" append to their study a chronological table, comprising "Recorded facts, deductions and traditions, relevant to the Play". This proves that they are close followers of the actual occurrences of Shakespeare's life, so far as they are certainly known; for it is true that more information is obtainable concerning our greatest dramatist than that given in the short passage from Steevens at the commencement of the book :—

" All we know with any degree of certainty concerning Shakespeare is that he was born at Stratford-upon

Avon, married and had children there; went to London, where he commenced as actor, and wrote poems and plays; returned to Stratford, made his will, died, and was buried ".

The question is rather, therefore, how far the character of Shakespeare, as conceived by them, is an accurate delineation. The writer of this criticism, while having the greatest admiration for the skill with which their conception is presented, is in agreement with the writer of the " Prefatory Note ". Shakespeare was too strong a personality to have yielded so easily to either the attractions or the disappointments of life, and his great tragedies are a proof that in Dowden's fine phrase he could go down " into the depths " of the human heart and yet keep his outlook on life clear and unembittered. The Shakespeare of " Lear " was the Shakespeare of " The Tempest ".

When criticising the picture of the poet as presented in the passionate drama of Miss Clemence Dane, it must not be forgotten that by entitling it " an invention " she has guarded herself against a demand for accuracy of fact. Leaving, therefore, the question of probability in event, let attention be concentrated on the person of the poet. " Will Shakespeare ", according to this authoress, is neither a strong nor noble character. He is cruel to his wife, easily swayed by passion and wavering in loyalty between his first and second love. He is an effective dramatic figure but hardly a living personality. This last criticism will also apply to the other characters of the drama ; Mary is light-of-love ; Elizabeth, vengeful and jealous ; and even Anne, who is the most pathetic, is more a voice than a reality. Compared

with Judith, Burbage, and Madame Montjoy in the
" Shakespeare ", they are indeed phantasmagorical.
It is not in the persons but in the poetry that the
greatness of Miss Dane's " Invention " lies. This
is often very fine, possessing music, power, balance
and inspiration, as the quotations given in this study
sufficiently prove. Added to the passionate emotion
that fills her lines is a realisation of the wonderful
effect produced by a suggestion of the supernatural,
as in the vision of Anne and the cry of the distant
child. The reader is chained by the beautiful verse
in a " Court of Romance lit by the flames of Love ".
" Will Shakespeare " belongs to the literature of
sensation rather than of thought, and in this field is
a fine and beautiful addition to our poetical drama.
Yet, in the field of realism, which is that of life, the
careful and scholarly work of Mr Rubinstein and Mr
Bax, stands no less high. It, too, is drama, if not
poetry; and its apparent simplicity should not blind
the reader to the art with which it is written. Both
plays are a notable effort to give to the present day
a vivid picture of our greatest dramatic poet, and
while one is painted in gorgeous colour and the other
finely drawn in black and white, they are both, art
and literature.

SOME ASPECTS OF SHAKESPEARE'S "RICHARD II" AND "HENRY V.".

A Lecture delivered at Highfield School, Watford.
May, 1923.

SOME ASPECTS OF SHAKESPEARE'S "RICHARD II" AND "HENRY V".

THE tragedy of fallen greatness and the praise of warrior courage are well-known themes for the poet and the dramatist. The history of every nation can furnish examples of desposed sovereignty and of brave endeavour against force; and Shakespeare, looking back at the end of the sixteenth century over the past of his country, could find in the troubled period between the death of Edward III and that of Henry VI, two kings whose reigns were the tale of diverted popularity and patriotic fervour. The contrast between his "Richard II" and his "Henry V" is not only that of the weak ruler and the eager conqueror, but between the lover of ease and the seeker for war, the man of thought and the man of action, the poet and the statesman. It is the realisation of different outlook and temperament, rather than the account of event and action, which give to this dramatist's historical plays their life and interest. It was during the age of Elizabeth that our English writers began to appreciate the wonderful pageantry of their nation's story, and the Chronicles of Stow and Holinshed, the poems of Drayton and Daniel, the "Edward II" of Marlowe, and the anonymous "Edward III", show how rich a field was furnished for the imaginative treatment of occurrence or annal. Shakespeare, therefore, in reviving with his genius the spirit of the past, was not working as a pioneer nor alone, but as part of his age, imbued with its love of England and her varied history. It is for this reason that we find him building so often on the writings of his predecessors and contemporaries. Holinshed is the framework for " Richard II " and " Henry V ", with hints in the first play from Froissart and Marlowe, and in the second from Hall and the " Famous Victories of Henry the Fifth ", an earlier production of unknown authorship. Shakespeare's originality is more in characterisation than in incident, and the first aspect of his genius may now be considered rather than the second, as the question of his sources of information, although a fascinating problem, is a study by itself.

The historical cycle of " Richard II ", " Henry IV " (1 and 2) and " Henry V ", covering a period of about fifty years, belongs to the first half of Shakespeare's life, and shows a development of style and treatment. In the opening tragedy the setting is almost entirely that of the Court, and the speakers of noble birth ; in the second we are introduced to the popular point of view, and the adventures of Falstaff are contrasted with the actions of Lords ; in the third we observe the poet's descriptive faculty predominating and his power of declamation at its height. If the first drama be the most poetical, the second is the most carefully balanced, and the third the most rapid in action. Surely something may be traced in this of the subtle instinct of the dramatist ; for in " Richard II " the luckless poet-king is the chief figure ; in " Henry IV " there is the relationship of the cool and calculating monarch to his undisciplined but politic son ; and in the last play, which voices the spirit of war, are given the inspired and inspiring Prologues, painting that which could not be presented

on the stage. It may also be noticed that in the
first tragedy Shakespeare avoids prose, in the second
confines it to the scenes of tavern life, but in the third
employs it for a speech of the King. Although it is
quite possible to consider the three plays separately
it must not be forgotten that their writer evidently
meant them to be consecutive,[1] and to this end has
developed the characters of Bolingbroke and of his
son. In " Richard II " the Duke of Hereford is first
pictured to the reader as a fiery-tempered knight,
eager to appeal Mowbray of treason and refusing to
be pacified by the King. This attitude is kept up
until his banishment in the lists at Coventry, where
almost his last words in the presence of Richard are
those of defiance. After the departure of the King,
however, he begins to realise his sentence, and in
reply to Gaunt's

> " All places that the eye of heaven visits,
>   Are to a wise man ports and happy havens ".[2]

answers :

> " O, no ; the apprehension of the good
>   Gives but the greater feeling to the worse ".[3]

and leaves emphasising his loyalty to his country.
The Henry of Lancaster who, returning, lands in
England during Richard's absence, is a politician as
well as a soldier, and throughout the rest of the
play, slowly increases his influence and power.
Shakespeare, however, is careful not to over-
emphasise his supremacy, and in the story of
Henry IV the difficulties with which he has to contend are described, not the least among them being
the behaviour of his son, to whom attention may

(1) " Richard II ", 1594. " Henry IV ", 1597. " Henry V ", 1599. (2)
" Richard II ", Act I, Sc. 3, 1.275. (3) " Richard II ", Act I, Sc. 3, 1.300.

now be directed. His life is displayed by his father in " Richard II " as one who

> " Daily doth frequent
> With unrestrained loose companions ",[1]

but also with some belief in his real worth:

> " As dissolute as desperate; yet through both
> I see some sparks of better hope, which elder years
> May happily bring forth ".[2]

In the succeeding drama are given vivid pictures of his life among the " tavern company ", as well as instances of the more serious side of his character. In " Henry V " he justifies the prophecy of Bolingbroke; and the King who answers, in the presence of his Council, the insult of the Dauphin, is a very different person from the participator in the Gadshill excursion. Two other points of treatment may be brought forward to prove Shakespeare's consistency of conception. That Henry the Fourth had faith in the efficacy of a pilgrimage to the Holy Land to pardon sin, is shown by his references to a crusade— as, for instance, at the end of " Richard II ":

> " I'll make a voyage to the Holy Land
> To wash this blood off from my guilty hand ",[3]

the opening of " Henry IV " and its close, where the dying King makes his pathetic request to be allowed to pass away in the Jerusalem Chamber. In the patriot King of " Henry V ", moreover, the dramatist has not forgotten the Prince of earlier days, and his exchange of a gage with Williams is an echo of the " Hal " that Falstaff knew. It is not possible in this place to treat the four dramas as a

(1) " Richard II ", Act V, Sc. 3, l. 6.   (2) Act V, Sc. 3, l. 20.   (3) Act V, Sc. 6, l. 49.

consecutive pageant of event and action; but in some analysis of the characterisation in the first and last the connecting historic links should be remembered.

The story of Richard the Second had, before the time of Shakespeare, been a theme in literature. Chaucer had addressed this King in the Envoy to one of his "Balades",[1] describing a Richard very different from that of the dramatist. Gower took the same attitude in his "Vox Clamantis";[2] and Langland, another contemporary of this unhappy monarch, refers to him in the Prologue to "Piers the Plowman",[3] while his poem on "Richard the Redeles", written about 1399,[3] advises the King to take his visitation of calamity in patience, touching also on the evils which he has brought upon his land. These last are the theme of another fourteenth century poem, of unknown authorship, on the "Deposition of Richard II".[4] There are, as well, two contemporary French accounts besides that of Froissart:[5] the first "Le Chronique de la Traison et Mort de Richart II",[6] and the second "L'Histoire du Roy d'Angleterre Richart".[7] Nearer to and in Shakespeare's own time there are the "Chronicles" of Fabian,[8] Hall,[9] Stow[10] and Holinshed;[11] the "Civil Wars" of Daniel,[12] and the "Edward II" of Marlowe,[13] dealing with a story akin to that of Richard. Shakespeare, therefore, had many sources on which to draw for his historical detail.

The play of "Richard II" belongs, as has been said, to the first part of the dramatist's life, and

(1) Works of Chaucer Oxford Edition, Ed. W. W. Skeat, p. 123.   (2) Gower, Works, Ed. by C. G. Macaulay; Oxford, 1902; Vol. 4, p. 230.   (3) Langland, "Piers the Plowman, etc.", Ed. W. W. Skeat, Vol. 1.   (4) Camden Soc., No. 3.   (5) "Chroniques", Paris, 1495 (?); trans. by Berners; 2 Vols., 1523, 1525.   (6) Eng. Hist. Soc.   (7) Webb, "Archælogia", No. 20.   (8) 1516, 33, 42, 59.   (9) 1548, 50.   (10) 1565 1575, 90.   (11) 1577, 86.   (12) Chalmers, Eng. Poets, Vol. 3.   (13) Plays of Marlowe; Ed. Dent; London, 1916; p. 225.

has been dated approximately 1594. The first quarto edition was published in 1597; but this, and that of 1598, exclude the crisis of the first scene in the fourth act—the yielding of the crown by Richard to Bolingbroke. It was, however, added in the third edition of 1608. The question of whether it was written earlier and suppressed, or composed for the first time for this quarto, has no certain answer, although probability would confirm the first assumption, nor is it even now decided if the poet were working on an older and inferior play, or only upon the " Chronicles ". The debt of Shakespeare to his contemporary Marlowe is no less than that to Holinshed. It takes the form of imitation of language and poetic construction[1] even more than suggestion of treatment. It may be noticed in passing that both dramatists seem fond of balancing clause with clause—a device probably derived from Lyly.[2]

The characterisation of Shakespeare's regal tragedy may now be considered. It might well bear upon its title page these lines from the historical drama of Marlowe—

> " But what are kings when regiment is gone
> But perfect shadows in a sunshine day ".[3]

It is the throwing of these shadows on the screen of imagination that exercises the genius of the two writers who, dealing with events of the same kind, interpret the chief actors in them differently. The similarity of incident in the plays is remarkable. In both the main figure alienates his barons by injustice, Edward confiscating the revenues of the Bishop of

(1) Cf. Rich. II, Act IV, Sc. 1, 1.285, with Marlowe. "Faustus", Ed. cit., p. 154. (2) "Euphr⁓s", 1579. (3) Marlowe, Ed. cit. "Ed. II", p. 277.

Coventry[1] and Richard those of John of Gaunt; and by insisting on their acceptance of the sovereign's favourites.[2] In each case the country, pillaged by taxes, is willing to rise against their imposers. Both monarchs are forced to resign their crowns in the presence of their nobles, subjected to indignity and finally murdered in obscurity.[3] Both dramas, moreover, have drawn their principal events from actual history. When, however, they are examined in further detail, the handling of their authors is seen to be individual. The period occupied by Marlowe's play is in reality twenty years, or the whole reign of Edward II, from which times he chooses the occurrences most suited to his conception of dramatic effect, and is more concerned with incident than with personality; Shakespeare, on the other hand, takes the poet's liberty of compressing months into days, and while according to the "Time-Analysis" of the play[4] the events take place in fourteen days, actually they were those of twenty-two months; the chief example occurring where Bolingbroke lands in England immediately after he has left it, whereas in reality he was absent nearly a year; this allows the dramatist to make the story more cogent, and what is of greater importance, to show the result of Richard's misplaced authority. Fine as are some of the speeches of Marlowe's King (that on his surrender of the crown bearing a similarity to the words of Richard on the occasion of a like act)[5] and powerful as is the description of his sufferings and death,[6] he seems more a stage-figure than a living person, and though he becomes human at the end of the play, when calamity

(1) Ed. II, p. 230.   (2) Rich. II, Act II, Sc. 1.   (3) Rich. II, Act IV, Sc. 1. Ed. II, p. 279.   Rich. II, Act V, Sc. 5. Ed. II, p. 291.   (4) "A Time-Analysis of Shakespeare's Plays". A. P. Daniel.   (5) Marlowe, Ed. II, p. 279.   Rich. II, Act IV, Sc. 1.   (6) Marlowe, Ed. cit., Ed. II, p. 291.

has broken down his obstinate and foolish pride, he is never a reality in the sense of the King of Shakespeare. Nor has this tragedy of " Edward II " any contrast of character; the nobles and Isabella are introduced as opposition to the weak ruler and his favourites, but seem to have little individuality; and for this reason the drama lacks balance and form, if not movement and force. (For instance, the scene in which the Lords demand the dismissal of Gaveston would be effective on the stage.)[1] To conclude— if Marlowe showed that the past could be re-pictured, Shakespeare proved it could be re-lived.

It is indeed the personality of Richard that lends the true interest to Shakespeare's conception of the ill-fated but not, therefore, ill-principled King; and while he did not seek to enter into a comparison with the tragic death-scene of Edward, he has given the story of a calamity no less moving. The historical background of the drama may be found in any study of the Plantaganet Period (1154-1485), and the incidents of the play shortly summarised. Richard, after striving to settle the dissension between Mowbray and Bolingbroke, appoints them a day of combat at Coventry. On that occasion, however, he stops the conflict and banishes the first for ever and the second for six years. He then visits his dying uncle, Gaunt, who reproaches him for his misrule and shortly afterwards dies, whereon the King seizes his estates for the expenses of the Irish wars, thus hastening his own downfall. He goes to Ireland and while absent the Queen learns of Bolingbroke's arrival in England, who advances successfully, the people rising to meet him. Richard returns to Wales, and, his forces having gone over to the invader, takes

(1) Marlowe, Ed. II, p. 249.

refuge in Flint Castle. He is approached here by
Bolingbroke who at first only claims his inheritance
from his father, Gaunt.   Finding that the King
submits, he brings him to London, and in the famous
deposition scene receives from him the crown. After
this Richard is taken to Pomfret Castle where he is
murdered, and the drama closes with the further
captures of Henry.

Shakespeare's interpretation of Richard's character seems to have been that he was a man of
personal courage but little judgment, with a poet's
capacity for creating pictures in his imagination. In
the first part of the play he visions himself in all the
pageantry of kingship, and does not realise that the
mere exercise of prerogative without force behind it
is both foolish and dangerous. This is shown in his
demand that Mowbray and Bolingbroke shall with-
draw their challenges to each other—

" Wrath-kindled gentlemen be ruled by me . . .
    Forget, forgive, conclude and be agreed "[1]

proving thus his entire lack of appreciation that their
honour was involved. When failing to achieve this
he appoints a day for their combat, he again speaks
in the most regal style, " We were not born to sue
but to command "[2] yet at the same time really con-
cedes to their wish. Having checked the contest,
he is evidently still imbued with the sense of his own
majesty, saying after having given sentence—

" Return again, and take an oath with thee.
    Lay on our royal sword your banish'd hands "[3]

but oblivious of the fact that his action has made
him two powerful enemies. In the scene where he

(1) Richard II, Act I, Sc. 1, l.153.   (2) Rich. II, Act I, Sc. 1, l.196.   (3)
Rich. II, Act I, Sc. 3, l.178.

mocks the dying Gaunt is shown how unkingly his sense of wounded pride can make him, and how blind he is to the danger in which he stands. When, moreover, he seizes the estates of his dead uncle, he is acting under the impression of the picture of the King conquering Ireland, and takes no notice of York's petition that he will reflect on what he does. He is next seen in Wales, apostrophising his kingdom in fanciful terms, stating that Heaven will defend him; then, however, comes successive bad news, until he suddenly realises that all is lost, and with imaginative quickness conjures up another picture—not that of the commanding ruler but that of the injured King. And this part he plays, not superficially, for he has convinced himself of its truth, but continuously until his death-hour, when he courageously attacks his murderers, yet is overcome. The tragedy of Richard lies in his unbalanced imagination which is displayed by the poet not only in his acts but in his wealth of simile and metaphor, his love of words and joy in playing with them. When the clear-headed Bolingbroke comments thus upon his victim's petulant breaking of the mirror—

" The shadow of your sorrow hath destroy'd
The shadow of your face "

Richard replies—

" Say that again—
The shadow of my sorrow; ha; let's see
'Tis very true, my grief lies all within ".[1]

Yet, after this scene he grows more calm, and when Northumberland enters to separate him from the Queen and lead him to Pomfret, his speech to him is both clearly phrased and full of shrewdness—

(1) " Richard II ", Act IV, Sc. 1, l.290.

" Northumberland, thou ladder wherewithal
    The mounting Bolingbroke ascends my throne . . ."[1]

Shakespeare who at first shows us a ruler to despise,
a King of words not deeds, gradually leads us to
realise the pathos of his position; and while Richard
is not a great tragic figure, he is a sadly human one.
It is impossible not to feel sorrow with the broken
heart that cries—

" I'll give my jewels for a set of beads,
    My gorgeous palace for a hermitage,
    My gay apparel for an almsman's gown,
    My figured goblets for a dish of wood,
    My sceptre for a palmer's walking-staff,
    My subjects for a pair of carved saints,
    And my large kingdom for a little grave,
    A little, little grave, an obscure grave . . ."[2]

and later, after trying to conquer loneliness with
ingenious but unsatisfying imagery—

" This music mads me; let it sound no more;
    For though it have holp madmen to their wits,
    In me it seems it will make wise men mad.
    Yet blessing on his heart that gives it me,
    For 'tis a sign of love—and love to Richard
    Is a strange brooch in this all-hating world ".[3]

One may condemn the King who could address
Gaunt—

" And thou—a lunatic lean-witted fool,
    Presuming on an ague's privilege,
    Dar'st with thy frozen admonition
    Make pale our cheek, chasing the royal blood
    With fury from his native residence ".[4]

(1) " Richard II ", Act V, Sc. 1, 1.55. (2) " Richard II ", Act III, Sc. 3,
1.147. (3) " Richard II ", Act V, Sc. 5, 1.61. (4) " Richard II ", Act II, Sc.
1, 1.115.

but pity the man who is forced to say—

> " I have no name, no title,
> No, not that name was given me at the font,
> But 'tis usurp'd; alack the heavy day
> That I have worn so many winters out,
> And know not now what name to call myself ".[1]

To this unfortunate character, to this imaginative mind capable of such true poetry as the lines—

> " For within the hollow crown
> That rounds the mortal temples of a King,
> Keeps Death his court, and there the antic sits,
> Scoffing his state and grinning at his pomp
> Allowing him a breath, a little scene
> To monarchize, be fear'd and kill with looks,
> Infusing him with self and vain conceit;
> As if this flesh which walls about our life
> Were brass impregnable, and humour'd thus
> Comes at the last and with a little pin
> Bores through his castle wall and—farewell King"[2]

is opposed Bolingbroke, at first, as has been said, high-spirited and eager for conflict, " a trueborn Englishman ", at a loss when banished how to live away from his country, and yet, even at this time, sarcastic as this couplet will prove—

> " Four lagging winters and four wanton springs
> End in a word—such is the breath of kings "[3]

Later, when he returns to claim his inheritance as a means to further influence, for he has by now learnt not to act hastily, his point of view has matured, the spirit and energy are still there but they are controlled by judgment and foresight. He knows that

(1) " Richard II ", Act IV, Sc. 1, 1.255. (2) " Richard II ", Act III, Sc. 2, 1.160. (3) " Richard II ", Act I, Sc. 3, 1.214.

time is on his side, and can afford to show attention
to Richard, from whom his broken oath had been
taken. There is fine irony in the scene at Flint
Castle—Richard knowing his weakness and trying to
brave it out—Bolingbroke knowing his strength and
playing the courtier. The last words of the King
and Duke are full of meaning—

BOLINGBROKE. " My gracious lord, I come but for
mine own.
    RICHARD. Your own is yours, and I am yours, and all.
    BOLINGBROKE. So far be mine my most redoubted lord
       As my true service shall deserve your love.
    RICHARD. Well you deserve; they well deserve to have
       That know the strong'st and surest way to get . . .
       Set on towards London, cousin, is it so?
    BOLINGBROKE. Yea, my good lord . . .
    RICHARD.   Then I must not say no ".[1]

Bolingbroke advances carefully. He speaks little but
promises more to the lords who join him on his arrival,
and is evidently pleased at their support, greeting
Hotspur—

    " I thank thee gentle Percy, and be sure
      I count myself in nothing else so happy
      As in a soul remembering my good friends ".[2]

He puts his case directly and clearly before the vacil-
lating Duke of York; and although the latter insists
on remaining neutral, knows that his sympathies are
with him rather than with Richard (Langley is Shakespeare's study in this play of the well-intentioned
man faced with problems above his power to solve).
Finally, Henry shows that he is determined to be
master, executing Bushy and Green, checking the
challenges of the nobles over Gloucester's death

(1) " Richard II ", Act III, Sc. 3, 1.200.   (2) " Richard II ", Act II, Sc. 3,
1.45.

(earlier in the play attributed, and rightly, by Gaunt to Richard's agency) with the words—

> " Lords appellants—
> Your differences shall all rest under gage,
> Till we assign you to your days of trial ".[1]

and arresting the Bishop of Carlisle when on Henry's—

> " In God's name I'll ascend the regal throne "[2]

he upholds in a fine speech the divine right of kings, ending with a prophecy—

> " O, if you raise this house against this house,
> It will the woefullest division prove
> That ever fell upon this cursed earth,
> Prevent it, resist it, let it not be so
> Lest child, child's children, cry against you 'woe' "[3]

(This ecclesiastic is, in fact, Richard's best advocate in the play.) The attitude which Bolingbroke takes in the " deposition scene " is outlined in the cold words—

> " Fetch hither Richard, that in common view
> He may surrender; so we shall proceed
> Without suspicion . . ."[4]

Throughout this wonderful passage, Shakespeare is careful to be consistent to the contrast in character between Henry and Richard. The former adopts a tone of patience tinged with scorn and his, " I thought you had been willing to resign ", " Are you contented to resign the crown ? "[5] cut across the eloquent imagery of the latter, who, feeling that he is playing his part of injured King, does not show any anger until the demand of Northumberland that he should

(1), (2), (3), (4), " Richard II ", Act IV, Sc. 1. (5) " Richard II ", Act IV, Sc. 1, L.200.

read aloud the account of his own crimes, rouses him
—" Fiend, thou torment'st me ere I come to Hell ";
Bolingbroke then says, " Urge it no more, my Lord
Northumberland ";[1] not probably from pity but lest
the Duke should take too much upon himself; and
Richard, after indulging in more symbolism and pro-
test, is led away, comforting himself perchance with
an ironic play upon words—

BOLINGBROKE. " Go, some of you convey him to the
Tower.
RICHARD. O, good; " convey ". Conveyers are you
all ".[2]

(Convey in Shakespeare's day had both the present
meaning and that of theft.) It is a powerful situation,
and while the reader dislikes Bolingbroke, he feels
his strength, and while despising Richard he pities
his humiliation. Bolingbroke is typical in the play of
judgment and power—Richard of pathos and poetry.
The other characters in the drama are less important. Gaunt is the wise and intensely patriotic noble
who, heartbroken at the state of his country, laments
it in the great outburst beginning—

" Methinks I am a prophet new inspired "

and including the well-known lines on England—

" This land of such dear souls, this dear, dear land ".[3]

This passage was re-printed in the anthology " England's Parnassus ".[4] One may regret the tendency
to word-play in a man with so much earnestness of
purpose, but this is little in comparison with the
courage and force of his rebuke to the King. The
character of Northumberland has been summarised

(1) " Richard II ", Act IV, Sc. 1, 1.271.   (2) " Richard II ", Act IV, Sc. 1,
1.317.   (3) " Richard II ", Act II, Sc. 1, 1.31.   (4) " England's Parnassus ". 1600.

by Richard in the speech quoted on an earlier page, and that of Mowbray is not important save as a foil to Bolingbroke at the opening of the tragedy. York and Carlisle have already been mentioned, and Salisbury is one of Richard's few adherents. The conspiracy and pardon of Aumerle are not essential to the story save in so far as they throw fresh light on the characters of York and of Henry. The Queen, although a pathetic, is a minor figure, and her introduction into the tragedy an instance of Shakespeare's invention. To the poet's imagination also is owing the kind-hearted gardener who says :

> " Here did she fall a tear, here in this place
> I'll set a bank of rue, sour herb of grace,
> Rue, even for ruth, here shortly shall be seen
> In the remembrance of a weeping queen ".[1]

and the faithful groom seeking his master in distress. The dramatist has wrought all these lesser persons with care and skill, but the story still remains that of Richard's fall, Bolingbroke's rise, and Gaunt's patriotism. Although it is an early work of Shakespeare, showing in its excess of rime his less mature style, it is full of fine thought, of vivid imagery, and of human interest. Critical opinion may be divided on its merits, but it is indeed one more to add to Richard's " sad stories of the death of kings ".

" Henry V ", although founded on the same chronicle as " Richard II ", is a very different production to the earlier play. Whereas in the drama of fallen kingship the characters inter-act upon each other, in the panegyric of war they form a chorus to the person of the warrior-king. In " Richard II " the reader's attention is divided, in " Henry V " it is

(1) " Richard II ", Act III, Sc. 4.

concentrated on one figure who lives in history a soldier-sovereign.

" The Life of Henry the Fifth " was first published in its complete form in the Folio of 1623, although probably written (from the allusion to Essex in the Prologue to Act V) about 1599. In 1600, however, a draft of the play was produced by Thomas Millington and John Bushy, and printed by Thomas Creede, entitled " The Cronicle History of Henry the Fift with his battell fought at Agin Court in France. Togither with Auntient Pistoll ".[1] This is not the drama as printed in the Folio, it is shorter, less polished and omits the magnificent prologues. It is a question among critics whether it formed the first sketch by Shakespeare for the longer play, or was a pirated copy from a stage performance of the whole, the exclusions and alterations being due to the transcriber. Modern opinion inclines to the latter view. Besides, Holinshed, which the dramatist followed often word for word, as in the exposition of Henry's claim to the French throne by the Archbishop of Canterbury (an argument historically ingenious, but ethically unsound)[2] he appears to have been familiar with a play published in 1598, and printed, curiously enough, by Thomas Creede, called " The Famous Victories of Henry the Fifth, conteining the honorable Battell of Agincourt ".[3] This piece, which overlaps the second part of " Henry IV ", is also founded on Holinshed, but has furnished the dramatist with suggestions for five scenes, two of which have no counterpart in the " Chronicle ". These are " the description of the Tun of treasure ",[4] the Dauphin's

(1) Parallel Texts " Cronicle " & " Folio ", Ed. by B. Nicholson, Intro. by P. A. Daniel. N.S. Soc. (2) " Henry V ", Act I, Sc. 2, l.33. (3) " Shakespeare's Library ", Ed. by W. C. Hazlitt; Vol. 5, p. 322. " Famous Victories ". (4) H.V., Act I, Sc. 2, l.254; F.V., p. 352.

scornful references to Henry,[1] the capture of Monsieur
le Fer by Pistol,[2] the negotiations between the French
and English Kings,[3] and, perhaps most important of
all, the wooing scene of Henry and Katharine.[4] There
are also in this play reminiscences of Lyly, as in the
simile of the bees[5] and several phrases in the speech
of Burgundy.[6] Shakespeare, in the " Life of Henry
the Fifth ", has again used his poet's prerogative to
compress time, for the events recorded in reality
cover a period of six years (1414-1420), and include
the two invasions of France in 1415 and 1417.

The dramatist has given indeed a series of pictures
from this space of time, and the characters seem to
fall into three divisions. The actions of Henry and
his nobles are contrasted with those of the French
King and his lords, and these themselves placed in
relation to the common soldier. The three aspects
of the struggle meet in the fourth act of the drama,
and in order to link the incidents together and to
thrill his audience with patriotic admiration of the
warrior-prince the poet composed the choruses to
each act, calling upon the imagination of his hearers
to visualise the passage of events.

> " Suppose that you have seen
> The well-appointed King at Hampton pier
> Embark his royalty. . . . Follow, follow—
> Grapple your minds to sternage of this navy—
> Work, work your thoughts, and therein see a
> siege . . ."[7]

The choruses, therefore, magnificent in themselves
as historic painting, are important as linking up the

(1) H.V., Act II, Sc. 4, 1.28; F.V., p. 357. (2) H.V., Act IV, Sc. 3; F.V.,
p. 368. (3) H.V., Act V, Sc. 2; F.V., p. 369. (4) H.V., Act V, Sc. 2; F.V.,
p. 371 (5) H.V., Act I, Sc. 2; Lyly; ed. Bond; Vol. 2, p. 44. (6) H.V., Act V,
Sc. 2. (7) " Henry V ", Prol. Act III, 1.3, 17, 25.

somewhat scattered scenes of the play. Shakespeare
knew well that it was impossible to fashion the story
of a war with its preparations and battles into such
a cogent interplay of character and action as
his " Richard II ". The whole drama is really
dependent on the aims and personality of Henry,
and the interpretation given by the writer to these
has been touched upon at the beginning of this paper.
Round the straight-forward facts of the English King
laying claim to the French throne, besieging Harfleur,
winning Agincourt, and wooing the daughter of the
French monarch, Shakespeare has built the Court and
battle speeches of this history. In the adventures of
Pistol and his companions he has shown the lighter
and meaner side of war. Some of the most striking
scenes in this epic-drama may now be touched upon
—the reception of the challenge from the Dauphin
and the reply,[1] the arrest of the traitors,[2] the talk
with the soldiers before Agincourt, and the famous
outburst of Henry to Westmoreland,[3] these are but
a few of the vivid incidents in this pageant of
patriotism, of colour, and of movement. How
grandly the newly-enthroned King replies to the
sarcastic insult of the French prince, when, through
the ambassadors, he sends as—

> " meeter for your spirit
> This tun of treasure; and in lieu of this
> Desires you let the dukedoms that you claim
> Hear no more of you. This the Dauphin speaks.
> K. HENRY. What treasure, uncle?
> EXETER.   Tennis-balls, my liege.
> K. HENRY. We are glad the Dauphin is so pleasant
>   with us;

(1) H.V., Act I, Sc. 2.   (2) " Henry V ", Act II, Sc. 2.   (3) H.V., Act IV.
Sc, 1, Sc, 3,

His present and your pains we thank you for,
When we have match'd our rackets to these balls
We will in France, by God's grace, play a set
Shall strike his father's crown into the hazard ".[1]

They indeed justify the warning of the Constable of
France—

" O peace, Prince Dauphin;
You are too much mistaken in this king ".[2]

How skilfully he leads the perjured Knights to their
own undoing, who, having shown no mercy, receive
none. There is a mingling of disappointed trust and
kingly dignity in Henry's reproach of his fallen
friends, and while his final address to them, " God
quit you in His mercy ",[3] is modelled on Holinshed,
the note of disillusionment is Shakespeare's own. In
the conversation between the King, Bates, and
Williams, wherein the dramatist shows his mastery
of prose, the reader is struck by the forcible argument
put forward by the last named speaker, which causes
Henry, in spite of his reply, " Every subject's duty
is the king's, but every subject's soul is his own ",[4]
to have some misgivings over the enterprise he has
undertaken, and his fine prayer has the accents of
remorse—

" O God of battles; Steel my soldiers' hearts . . .
Not to-day, O Lord,
O, not to-day, think Thou upon the fault
My father made in compassing the crown . . .
I Richard's body have interred new . . ."[5]

This, however, has left him in the speech before
Agincourt—

(1) " Henry V ", Act I, Sc. 2, 1.255; F.V., Ed. cit., p. 352. (2) H.V., Act II,
Sc. 4, 1.30; Cf., F.V., p. 357. (3) " Henry V ", Act II, Sc. 3, Holinshed, Ed. cit.
(Shakespeare's Holinshed, ed. W. G. Boswell-Stone), p. 548. (4) " Henry V ",
Act IV, Sc. 1, 1.184. (5) H.V., Act IV, Sc. 1, 1.205.

" If we are mark'd to die, we are enow
  To do our country loss; and if to live
  The fewer men the greater share of honour ".[1]

It is a play full of the finest declamatory poetry, and
passage after passage rings with the clear note of the
herald's trumpet. It contains little pathos, with the
exception perhaps of the tale of the deaths of Suffolk
and York: " A testament of noble-ending love ",[2]
and the spirit of reflection is largely absent. Before
passing on to a conclusion, something must be said
of the French scenes, and those in which Pistol, Bardolph, Nym and Falstaff's boy, argue and wrangle.
The former are evidently introduced by the dramatist
as a foil to the English, but with the exception of the
King, who is a stately figure, and the Duke of Burgundy, they are not of much interest, and the reader
grows tired of the Dauphin and his horse. The
Princess, however, is a delicately sketched figure, and
Shakespeare fulfils the promise given in the Epilogue
to " Henry IV ", " to make you merry with fair
Katharine of France ".[3] The latter scenes are really
the outcome of those which occur in " Henry IV ",
and the persons of Pistol, Bardolph, and the Boy,
survive from the earlier drama. None of these rogues
is as entertaining as Falstaff, and the writer appears to
have introduced them among the greater figures either
to please the less educated of his audience or to form
a contrast. There is one minor individual, however,
on whom Shakespeare has spent much care, namely,
Fluellen, a further study of the Welshman as pre-
viously outlined in Owen Glendower. This versatile
Captain is as much at home describing the exploits
of the Duke of Exeter at the " Pridge ", as making

(1) H.V., Act IV, Sc. 3, l.20.   (2) H.V., Act IV, Sc. 4, l.27.   (3) " Henry IV ", Epilog., Part II.

Pistol eat the leek which he has abused. He is indeed a link between the Court and the Camp, and Henry's description of him is happy—

" Though it appear a little out of fashion
  There is much care and valour in this Welchman ".[1]

The reader certainly agrees that " to kill the poys and the luggage 'tis expressly against the law of arms ".[2] After all, however, this drama remains the pageant of the warrior-prince, the hero of Agincourt, and the conqueror of France.

Yet vivid as Shakespeare has made the scenes of this history, his genius shines brightest in the varied music of the chorus. And even if rhetorical, what splendid music it is, so different from the wayward poetry of Richard or the cold statement of Bolingbroke. The opening appeal to the spirit of imagination—

" O, for a Muse of fire, that would ascend
  The brightest heaven of invention . . ."[3]

the doubt—

                    " Can this cockpit hold
  The vasty fields of France? Or may we cram
  Within this wooden O, the very casques
  That did affright the air at Agincourt? "[4]

so triumphantly answered by this gift, the description of the preparation—

" Now all the youth of England are on fire
  And silken dalliance in the wardrobe lies . . .
  For now sits Expectation in the air . . ."[5]

the sketch of assault—

(1) " Henry V ", Act IV, Sc. 1, l.83. (2) Act IV, Sc. 7. (3) " Henry V "
Chorus, Act I, l.1. (4) Chorus, Act I, l.11. (5) " Henry V ", Chorus, Act II, l.1.

" and the nimble gunner
With linstock now the devilish cannon touches . . .
    (Alarum)
And down goes all before them . . ."[1]

the night of waiting—

" When creeping murmur and the poring dark
Fills the wide vessel of the universe.
From camp to camp through the foul womb of night
The hum of either army stilly sounds,
That the fix'd sentinels almost receive
The secret whispers of each other's watch ".[2]

and the account of the victor's return—

" You may imagine him upon Blackheath,
Where that his lords desire him to have borne
His bruised helmet and his bended sword
Before him through the city; he forbids it
Being free from vainness and self-glorious pride,
Giving full trophy, signal and ostent
Quite from himself, to God ".[3]

all are built

" In the quick forge and working-house of thought "[4]

Sir Philip Sidney, himself a hero and a poet, confessed, " I never heard the old song of Percy and Douglas, that I found not my heart moved more than with a trumpet ";[5] cannot the same be said of this epic of patriotism and its eulogy enshrined in its own Epilogue—

" Thus far, with rough and all unable pen
Our bending author hath pursu'd the story;
In little room confining mighty men,
Mangling by starts the full course of their glory.
Small time, but in that small most greatly liv'd
This star of England " ?[6]

(1) Chorus, Act III.   (2) " Henry V ", Chorus, Act IV.   (3) " Henry V ", Chorus, Act V.   (4) " Henry V ", Chorus Act V.   (5) " Apology for Poetry "; Ed. Magnus; p. 70.   (6) " Henry V ", Epilogue.

CHRISTOPHER MARLOWE
AS A POET.

A Paper read before the Discussion Society of the School of English Literature at Oxford. 1919. The late Sir Walter Raleigh in the Chair.

CHRISTOPHER MARLOWE
AS A POET.

" He who erewhile wrote with a brand of fire—
Now, in his passionate blood, floats t'ward the grave;
The present time is ever ignorant,
We lack clear vision in our self-love's maze.
But Marlowe in the future will stand great,
Whom this—the lowest caitiff in the world
A nothing, save in grossness hath destroyed ".[1]

In these lines from Horne's pathetic tragedy, " The Death of Marlowe ", the dramatist Middleton pays his tribute of honour to the dying poet, as he lies struck by the dagger of a tavern pander, Jaconot, whose mistress, Cecilia, he has worshipped as a saint. This version of his death is as probable as any other, for not only the end, but the greater part of Marlowe's life, is wrapped in uncertainty and doubt. All that is known may be shortly told. " Born in 1564 of poor parents in Canterbury, he was educated at the King's School there, and in 1581 went to Benet's (now Corpus Christi) College, Cambridge, probably through the munificence of Sir Roger Manwood, on whom, in later life, he wrote a Latin Epitaph. In 1583 he took his B.A. Degree, and in 1587 that of M.A. On leaving the University, it is possible he saw service in the Low Countries, as he shows some familiarity with military terms, but from this time, until his death in 1593, nothing definite is known ".[2] It is strange that

(1) Horne. " Death of Marlowe ". 1837. Quoted by A. H. Bullen. (2) Cousin's Biographical Dict. of Eng. Lit. " Everyman ". 1012.

CHRISTOPHER MARLOWE AS A POET.

although he was the author of an exceedingly popular play, there are few references, and those unfavourable, to him during his life, the chief being the long reproach of his actions and atheism in Greene's "Groat's Worth of Wit"; and an exaggerted account in the form of " A note delivered on Whitson Eve last of the horrible blasphemies uttered by Cristofer Marly who, within three days after, came to a sudden and fearful end of his life ", written by an unknown hand.[1] Shortly after his death, however, many eulogies were composed on the young, ill-fated dramatist who " swept from the English stage the tatters of barbarism and habited Tragedy in stately robes ".[2] The finest is this noble panegyric of Drayton—

> " Next Marlowe, bathed in the Thespian springs,
> Had in him those brave translunary things
> That the first poets had; his raptures were
> All air and fire, which made his verses clear;
> For that fine madness still he did retain
> Which rightly should possess a poet's brain ".[3]

" A poet's brain "—this is indeed true of Marlowe, who was a poet by nature and a dramatist by necessity. It is poetic imagination that causes all his dramas, with the possible exception of " Edward II ", which is his most mature, and probably last-written, play to be more a collection of magnificent scenes than the steady development of a story. It is in these brilliant fragments, often so lightly strung together, that Marlowe expresses his deepest and most noble thoughts, in language which sweeps on in a majestic flow, until the mind is overwhelmed by the torrent of image, of simile and of beauty. - Poetry,

(1) Circa, 1592. (2) Bullen. (3) Drayton; Ep. to H. Reynolds; c.1627.

vision and power combine in one grand symphony, and the poet becomes in truth " a mighty-mouthed inventor of harmonies ". Such are the beauties of Marlowe's earlier work, but " later he learned to breathe sweetness and softness into his mighty line, to make the measure that had thundered the threats of Tamburlaine falter the sobs of a broken heart ".[1] Then while the death of Faustus fills us with a sense of terror, that of Edward wakes the feeling of pity, and we know that the poet realises that " he has seen but half the universe who has never been shown the house of Pain ".[2] Is it possible that before Marlowe wrote his greatest play he had passed through some deep personal sorrow, leaving its impression on his work?

If the poetic instinct be stronger than the dramatic in Marlowe it may be expected that when he leaves the characterisation of the stage for the freedom of the lyric, his verse will attain to its greatest beauty, and as poetry which fulfils the definition of Leigh Hunt, " It is a passion for beauty, because its office is to exalt and refine by means of pleasure, and because beauty is nothing but the loveliest form of pleasure ",[3] it undoubtedly does so, for what it loses in power it gains in inspiration. Swinburne has well said of Marlowe's " Hero and Leander " that it " stands out alone amid all the wild and poetic wealth of its teeming and turbulent age as might a small shrine of Parian sculpture amid the rank splendour of a tropic jungle ",[4] and a later critic confirms this when he says, " the rich music of 'Hero and Leander' was heard no more in England till the coming of Keats ".[5] " The rest of Shakespeare's predecessors are shadows—Marlowe alone lives ".[5]

(1) Bullen. (2) Emerson, Essays. (3) Leigh Hunt, " Imagination and Fancy ". (4) Swinburne. (5) Bullen, " Works of Marlowe ", 3 Vols., 1885.

The reference in this passage to Keats is of interest, for, in the works of Marlowe and of the later poet, there are points of resemblance. Both died before thirty; in both there was a development of genius, and in both a passionate love of beauty; the luxuriance of "Tamburlaine" gave place to the restraint of "Edward II", and the inequality of "Endymion" was succeeded by the majesty of "Hyperion". Keats, though the greater poet, was equalled by Marlowe in his love of classical mythology, and such lines as—

> " Thy bright team
> Gulfs in the morning light, and scuds along
> To bring thee nearer to that golden song
> Apollo singeth, while his chariot
> Waits at the doors of heaven "[1]

from " Endymion ", and—

> " By this Apollo's golden harp began
> To sound forth music to the ocean,
> Which watchful Hesperus no sooner heard
> But he the bright Day-bearing car prepared ".[2]

from "Hero and Leander", show not only a similarity of thought, but also of expression. This note of beauty runs through all the work of Marlowe, and may be found in the plays no less than in the poems. In "Tamburlaine", for instance, the impression given is one of gorgeous Eastern pageantry, and although the poem, for it is more a poem than a play, is filled with much extravagance of diction and an excess of declamation, there are many passages of real, and sometimes of great poetry. The beautiful descriptions of Zenocrate—

(1) " Endymion ", Book III. (2) " Hero and Leander ", Sestiad II.

" Zenocrate, lovelier than the love of Iove,
 Brighter than is the silver Rhodophe,
 Fairer than whitest snow on Scythian hills ".[1]

" Zenocrate, the loveliest maid alive,
 Fairer than rocks of pearl and precious stone,
 Whose eyes are brighter than the lamps of heaven,
 And speech more pleasant than sweet harmony ".[2]

show how easily similes flow in upon Marlowe, when he abandons himself to the simple description of beauty, while the thoughts expressed in the noble speech of Tamburlaine—

" Nature, that framed us of four elements
 Warring within our breasts for regiment,
 Doth teach us all to have aspiring minds;
 Our souls, whose faculties can comprehend
 The wondrous architecture of the world,
 And measure every wandering planet's course,
 Still climbing after knowledge infinite,
 And always moving as the restless spheres,
 Will us to wear ourselves, and never rest,
 Until we reach the ripest fruit of all,
 That perfect bliss and sole felicity . . ."[3]

are a magnificent expression of the " devotion to something afar from the sphere of our sorrow ",[4] are worthy of Shakespeare, and would not be out of place in " Hamlet ". But Marlowe, in his desire to link this passage with the character of his hero, adds a line, making the " sole felicity " the " sweet fruition of an earthly crown ", an anti-climax unworthy both of the poet and of his genius. These are perhaps the finest lines in the work, but there are others which, if less noble in conception, show the descriptive power

(1) " Tamburlaine ", I, Act I Sc. 2. (2) " Tamburlaine ", I, Act III, Sc. 3.
(3) " Tamburlaine ", I, Act II, Sc. 7 (Dyce). (4) Shellev. " To —— ".

more clearly. Such are the verses in which Marlowe describes a night of storm—

> " Let ugly Darkness with her rusty coach
> Engirt with tempests, wrapt in pitchy clouds,
> Smother the earth with never-fading mists,
> And let her horses from their nostrils breathe
> Rebellious winds and dreadful thunder-claps "[1]

and those wherein he writes of—

> " The golden ball of heaven's eternal fire
> That danced with glory on the silver waves ".[2]

Before leaving this poem two other interesting quotations may be given. It is in " Tamburlaine " that occur the well-known lines—

> " If all the pens that ever poets held
> Had fed the feeling of their master's thoughts,
> And every sweetness that inspired their hearts,
> Their minds and muses on admirèd themes;
> If all the heavenly quintessence they still
> From their immortal flowers of poesy,
> Wherein, as in a mirror, we perceive
> The highest reaches of a human wit;
> If these had made one poem's period,
> And all combined in beauty's worthiness—
> Yet should there hover in their restless heads
> One thought, one grace, one wonder at the least
> Which into words no virtue can digest "[3]

wherein Marlowe praises the beauty which is indescribable. The first version, moreover, of the famous passage in " Faustus " where the Doctor addresses the shade of Helen as " Was this the face which launched a thousand ships ? "[4] is probably to be found in these lines—

(1) " Tamburlaine ", I, Act V, Sc. 1. (2) " Tamburlaine ", II, Act II, Sc. 4.
(3) " Tamburlaine ", Act V, Sc. 1. (4) " Faustus ", Sc. XIV.

" Helen, whose beauty summon'd Greece to arms,
     And drew a thousand ships to Tenedos ".[1]

The dramatic poem of " Tamburlaine " was shortly
followed by the far greater work of " Faustus ".
The subject was exactly fitted to the temperament
of Marlowe, and, with the exception of some comic
scenes, which, as Bullen says, are probably spurious,
the story steadily increases in power, until tragedy,
remorse and mental agony meet in the last speech of
Faustus.[2]   The foundation of Marlowe's greatest
psychological drama was a translation from a German
History of Dr. Faustus, published in 1592, a work of
some length and containing many fine passages, yet
unworthy of comparison with the play to which it
gave rise.   The spirit of Marlowe's drama is different
to that of the History, wherein the motive for the
compact with Lucifer is a desire for worldly pleasure,
for in the play the Doctor desires power to control
supernatural forces—

" Shall I make spirits fetch me what I please,
     Resolve me of all ambiguities,
     Perform what desperate enterprise I will?
     I'll have them fly to India for gold,
     Ransack the ocean for orient pearl
     And search all corners of the new-found world ".[3]

This play, more than any other of Marlowe's, is filled
with magnificent poetry.   Leaving the last speech of
Faustus, in which the poet reaches his highest summit
of imaginative horror, wherein the short and agonised
sentences follow each other like the ticking of the
clock which brings nearer the moment of doom, as
too long for quotation,[4] there are several lines which
few other poets could have written ; such are—

(1) " Tamburlaine ", II, Act II, Sc. 4. (2) " Faustus ", 1st Ed., 1604; " Faust-
buch ", 1587; " Ballad of Faustus ", 1589.   (3) " Faustus ", Sc. 1.   (4)
" Faustus ", Sc. XVI.

" Have I not made blind Homer sing to me
Of Alexander's love, and Aenon's death ? "

" So shall the spirits of every element
Be always serviceable to us three,
Sometimes like women, or unwedded maids
Shadowing more beauty in their airy brows
Than have the white breasts of the queen of love ".

" O thou art fairer than the evening air
Clad in the beauty of a thousand stars ".[1]

and the fine account of—
                    " the restless course
That Time doth run with calm and silent foot,
Shortening my days and thread of vital life—

and of night—

" Now that the gloomy shadow of the earth
Longing to view Orion's drizzling look,
Leaps from th'antarctic world into the sky
And dims the welkin with her pitchy breath ".[2]

Marlowe's version is the first great tragedy founded
on this story; nor did any until the time of Goethe
venture on a fresh handling of the theme, but he, an
intense admirer of Marlowe, re-cast the legend and
gave to the world his " Faust ".[3] The German poet
has extended the tale with much lovely and noble
lyrical verse, but while he has created the gentle
and lovely Marguerite, and has described with vividness the Walpurgis Night, he refrains from entering
into comparison with the earlier poet's final scene,
his conclusion to the drama being different and far
less impressive. The story has, moreover, formed the
basis of the best operas of Gounod[4] and Berlioz.[5]

(1) and (2) " Faustus ", Sc. VI, Sc. I, Sc XIV, Sc. XI, Sc. III. (3) " Faust ",
1806. (4) Gounod, 1859. (5) Berlioz, 1880.

Many lines in this play may have had their influence on later poetry as, for instance, Milton's—

" Is this the region, this the soil, the clime,
    Said then the lost Archangel, this the seat,
    Then we must change for heaven, this mournful gloom
    For that celestial light ? "[1]

possibly suggested by the following from Marlowe—

" Why, this is hell, nor am I out of it,
    Think'st thou that I who saw the face of God
    And tasted the eternal joys of heaven
    Am not tormented with ten thousand hells ? "[2]

Many passages in the first two books of " Paradise Lost " and certainly the digression on astronomy at the beginning of the eighth, were presaged by those parts of the tragedy where Faustus and Mephistophiles reason concerning Hell and the Celestial motions. Browning also may have had Marlowe in his mind when he wrote of his Paracelsus, who like the latter's Faustus, had attained great fame and reputation for wisdom, and made him say—

" I have dared, come to a pause with knowledge;
                and here amid the scrawled
    Uncouth recordings of the dupes of this
    Old arch genethliac, lie my life's results ".

" A few blurred characters suffice to note
    The fragmentary produce of much toil;
    And yet those blottings chronicle a life—
    A whole life and my life "[3]

for the lines recall those of the earlier magician—

(1) Milton, " Paradise Lost ", Book I, l.242. (2) " Faustus ", Sc. III. (3) " Paracelsus ", II.

" Why, Faustus, hast thou not attain'd that end?
Is not thy common talk found aphorisms?
Are not thy bills hung up a monuments
Whereby whole cities have escaped the plague
And thousand desperate maladies been eas'd?
Yet art thou still but Faustus, and a man ".[1]

Marlowe's next play is of a different type. " The
Jew of Malta " personifies the lust for wealth, and
the description, given by Barabas at the commencement of the play, of his riches, is very fine.[2] The
continuation of the story, however, is unworthy of
the opening, and the Jew with whom we have some
sympathy when his wealth is seized by the Governor
of Malta, loses our interest when we find in the words
of Lamb that " Barabas is a mere monster. . . . He
kills in sport, poisons whole nunneries, invents
infernal machines ", and even murders his own
daughter.[3] Shylock is, in spite of his cruelty, a
human being—

" Fed with the same food, hurt with the same
weapons, subject to the same diseases, healed by the
same means, warmed and cooled by the same winter and
summer as a Christian is "[4]

and our sympathy is with him in the loss of Jessica,
and when he leaves the court broken with sorrow, " I
pray you, give me leave to go from hence—I am not
well "[5] we pity a worn-out old man. But Barabas
is a figure, nothing more, into whom Marlowe has
breathed the spirit of hate, to please the popular
conception of his day—that a Jew was the incarnation of evil. The play, therefore, has but little

(1) "Faustus", Sc. I. (2) "Jew of Malta"; acted, 1591. (3) Lamb's "Dramatic
Specimens". (4) " Merchant of Venice ", Act III, Sc. 1. (5) " Merchant of
Venice ", Act IV, Sc. 1.

interest, save in some fine descriptive passages, such as—

> " Why then I hope my ships
> I sent for Egypt and the bordering isles,
> Are gotten up by Nilus winding banks;
> Mine argosy from Alexandria,
> Loaden with spice and silks, now under sail
> Are smoothly gliding down by Candy-shore
> To Malta, through our Mediterranean sea "[1]

A quotation which in its employment of sonorous names suggest the lines of Milton—

> " Sea had he searched and land
> From Eden over Pontus and the pool
> Maeotis up beyond the river Ob;
> Downward as far antarctic; and in length
> West from Orontes to the ocean barr'd
> At Darien "[2]

and the rich description of wealth—

> " Bags of fiery opals, sapphires, amethysts,
> Jacinths, hard topaz, grass-green emeralds,
> Beauteous rubies, sparkling diamonds,
> And seld-seen costly stones of so great price,
> Infinite riches in a little room "[3]

and, finally, the description of the ill-omened bird—

> " Thus, like the sad presaging raven, that tolls
> The sick man's passport in her hollow beak,
> And in the shadow of the silent night
> Doth shake contagion from her sable wings ".[4]

" The Massacre at Paris ", another tragedy of Marlowe's, is injured by its foundation on a nearly contemporary event, for the incidents took place in 1572, and the play was produced in 1592. It is a tale

(1) " Jew of Malta ", Act I, Sc. 1. (2) " Paradise Lost ", Book IX, l.80. (3) " Jew of Malta ", Act I, Sc. 1. (4) " Jew of Malta ", Act II, Sc. 1.

of murders, and with the exception of a fine but terribly cruel speech of the Duke of Guise, contains little dramatic power or real poetry. The death scene of this nobleman is of interest as it contains the courageous words—

> " Yet Cæsar shall go forth—
> Let mean conceits and baser men fear death,
> Tut, they are peasants; I am Duke of Guise,
> And princess with their looks engender fear,
> Thus Cæsar did go forth and thus he died ".[1]

which are almost identical with those of Shakespeare's Emperor—

> " Cæsar shall forth, the things that threaten'd me
> Ne'er look'd but on my back; when they shall see
> The face of Cæsar, they are vanished "[2]

but the final lines, spoken by King Henry the Third, in this play are greatly inferior in beauty, poetry and pathos to those of Marlowe's " Edward II ". Before passing on to this tragedy—the most restrained and mature of his work—some fine similes in the " Massacre at Paris " may be mentioned. Guise says—

> " Give me a look that when I bend the brows
> Pale death may walk in furrows of my face "[3]

and describes the approaching night of slaughter—

> " If ever Hymen lour'd at marriage-rites,
> And had his altars deck'd with dusky lights;
> If ever sun stain'd heaven with bloody clouds,
> And made it look with terror on the world;

(1) " Massacre at Paris ", 1592, Sc. XXI.   (2) " Julius Cæsar ", Act II, Sc. 2.
(3) " Massacre at Paris ", Sc. II.

> If ever day were turned to ugly night,
> And night made semblance of the hue of hell;
> This day, this hour, this fatal night,
> Shall fully show the fury of them all ".[1]

The historical drama of " Edward II " has often been compared with that of " Richard II ", and the comparison is fair and of much interest. Lamb has well said of this play : " This tragedy is in a very different style from mighty ' Tamburlaine '. The reluctant pangs of abdicating royalty in Edward, furnished hints which Shakespeare scarce improved in his ' Richard II ', and the death-scene of Marlowe's king moves pity and terror beyond any scene, ancient or modern, with which I am acquainted ".[2] The close resemblance to which he refers occurs in the fourth act of Shakespeare's play and the fifth of Marlowe's, and in reading these the former is seen to have pathos, but the latter power—Richard, a poet by nature, and a king by fate—piles up simile upon simile, and with imaginative anguish calls for a glass in which to see his suffering—

> " Hath sorrow struck
> So many blows upon this face of mine
> And made no deeper wounds ?
> A brittle glory shineth in this face,
> As brittle as the glory, is the face ".[3]

Edward, more resentful and less sensitive, bitterly reviles his deposers, saying of the crown—

> " Take it. What, are you mov'd, pity you me ?
> Then send for unrelenting Mortimer,
> And Isabel, whose eyes, being turn'd to steel
> Will sooner sparkle fire than shed a tear "[4]

(1) " Massacre at Paris ", Sc. II. (2) Lamb, " Dramatic Specimens ". (3) " Richard II ", Act IV, Sc. 1. (4) " Edward II ", Act V, Sc. I.

and throughout this scene the King speaks with a tone of defiance very different from the womanly surrender of Richard, who says—

  " With mine own tears I wash away my balm,
    With mine own hands I give away my crown,
    With mine own tongue deny my sacred state,
    With mine own breath release all duty's rites ".[1]

Edward, though in despair, braves his foes, crying—

  " Inhuman creatures, nurs'd with tiger's milk,
    Why gape you for your sovereign's overthrow ? "[2]

It is impossible to say which of these scenes is the finer; but the play of Shakespeare has the luxuriance of youth, that of Marlowe the restraint of maturity. The death of Edward surpasses, however, that of Richard in its accumulated tragedy, and in the helplessness of the royal victim, for while Richard, stirred for once from his reflections on life, seizes the axe from one of his would-be murderers and strikes at him with the words: " Villain, thy own hand yields thy death's instrument ", but afterwards, when dying by the hand of Exton, falls back into his introspective habit and laments that the country will suffer from his death, saying:

            " Exton thy fierce hand
  Hath with the King's blood stain'd the king's own land.
  Mount, mount, my soul; thy seat is up on high—
  Whilst my gross flesh sinks downward, here to die ".[3]

Edward II, deserted, tortured and starving, breaks forth with a pathos unknown to Richard—

  " But that grief keeps me waking, I should sleep
    For not these ten days have these eye-lids clos'd.
    Now, as I speak, they fall; and yet with fear
    Open again. O wherefore sitt'st thou there ".[4]

  (1) " Richard II ", Act IV, Sc. 1. (2) " Edward II ", Act V, Sc. 1. (3)
" Richard II ", Act V, Sc. 5. (4) " Edward II ", Act V, Sc. 5.

It is with such simple lines that Marlowe achieves immortality. Yet there are many other passages in this play, of which Shakespeare, even at his greatest heights, might have been proud, such are the laments of Edward—

> " Good father, on thy lap
>   Lay I this head laden with mickle care.
>   O, might I never ope these eyes again,
>   Never again lift up this drooping head,
>   O never more lift up this dying heart . . .
>   A litter hast thou? Lay me in a hearse
>   And to the gates of Hell convey me hence;
>   Let Pluto's bells ring out my fatal knell,
>   And hags howl for my death at Charon's shore;
>   For friends hath Edward none but these,
>   And these must die under a tyrant's sword "[1]

and the fine simile—

> " But what are kings when regiment is gone,
>   But perfect shadows in a sunshine day "[2]

while all the fire of Shakespeare's warrior-princes sounds in—

> " Come, uncle, let us leave the brain-sick king,
>   And henceforth parley with our naked swords "[3]

and in the words of Mortimer—

> " This tatter'd ensign of my ancestors,
>   Which swept the desert shore of that Dead Sea,
>   Whereof we got the name of Mortimer . . ."[4]

> " Farewell, fair queen, weep not for Mortimer
>   That scorns the world, and as a traveller
>   Goes to discover countries yet unknown ".[5]

Although Marlowe has little skill in portraying

(1) " Edward II ", Act IV, Sc. 6. (2) " Edward II ", Act V, Sc. 1. (3) " Edward II ", Act I, Sc. 1. (4) " Edward II ", Act II, Sc. 3. (5) " Edward II ", Act V, Sc. 6.

women, his Isabella shows a mother's love when she
says—

> " Ah, boy, this towardness makes thy mother fear,
> Thou art not mark'd to many days on earth ".[1]

These are a few of the many immortal passages
scattered through this great play, the greatest historical drama before the magnificent series of Shakespeare, wherein ninety years of our nation's story are
made to live before our eyes through the magic of his
genius.

With Edward II we may close the purely original
dramatic work of Marlowe, for although he collabor-
ated with Nash in his " Dido, Queen of Carthage ",
and with others, of whom one may have been Shakespeare in " The True Tragedy of Richard, Duke of
York ", it is a fruitless task to attempt an accurate
division of authorship. In both plays there are lines
of beauty and power worthy of Marlowe at his best,
as, for example, the final speech of Gloucester in
" The True Tragedies "—

> " And, father, do but think
> How sweet a thing it is to wear a crown
> Within whose circuit is Elysium
> And all that poets feign of bliss and joy ".[2]

Only the poet of " Hero and Leander " could have
written in " Dido " the lines—

> " Her silver arms will coll me round about,
> And tears of pearl cry, " Stay, Aeneas, stay ".[3]

> " And after him a thousand Greecians more
> In whose stern faces shin'd the quenchless fire
> That after burnt the pride of Asia "[4]

while those of the despairing Queen—

(1) " Edward II ", Act III, Sc. 2. " Dido, Queen of Carthage ". c. 1594. " True
Tragedie ", c. 1595. (2) " True Tragedie ", Act V, Sc. 7. (3) " Dido ", Act IV,
Sc. 4. (4) " Dido ", Act II, Sc. 1.

" O that I had a charm to keep the winds
   Within the closure of a golden ball,
   Or that the Tyrrhene sea were in my arms
   That he might suffer shipwreck on my breast . . .
   If he forsake me not, I never die
   For in his looks I see eternity,
   And he'll make me immortal with a kiss "[1]

contain an echo of the invocation to Helen by Faustus.
The whole play is a poem rather than a drama.

The quotations given from the dramatic work of
Marlowe in the preceding pages may serve two pur-
poses, for they may prove the statement made earlier
in this paper that he was a dramatist by necessity,
but a poet by nature, and may serve to call attention
to the many jewels adorning his plays, for these are
too often studied as the work of an Elizabethan playwright, rather than as that of a great sixteenth
century poet. His purely lyrical verses are few, but
no one, on reading his other compositions, can fail
to observe the predominance of this note. It occurs
in his translations from the Latin, no less than in his
plays and English poems. In these versions, often
inaccurate in detail, he catches the spirit of the
original, and some of his lines are quite as beautiful.
He has, for instance, translated—

" Stat vetus et multos incaedua silva per annos :
   Credibilest illi numen inesse loco;
   Fons sacer in medio sepluncaque pumice pendens,
   Et latere ex omni dulce queruntur aves ".[2]

as

" An old wood stands, uncut of long years' space,
   'Tis credible some god-head haunts the place,
   In midst thereof a stone-paved sacred spring,
   Where round about small birds most sweetly sing ".[3]

(1) " Dido ", Act IV, Sc. 4. (2) Ovid. " Amorum ", Bk. III, Eleg. 1. (3)
Marlowe, Bk. III, Eleg. 1.

and followed Ovid in praising Homer—

> " Adice, Maeonidem a quo ceu fonte perenni
> Vatum Pieriis ora rigantur aquis ".

> " See Homer, from whose fountain ever filled
> Pierian dew to poets is distilled "[1]

rendering a phrase which might well apply to himself—

> " Scindentur vestes; gemmae frangentur et aurum
> Carmina quam tribuent, fama perennis erit ".

as

> " Garments do wear, jewels and gold do waste,
> The fame that verse gives doth for ever last ".[2]

Nor does the description of Juno's festival, in Ovid's thirteenth Elegy of the third book, lose any of its gaiety in his translation. Marlowe's version of the First Book of Lucan is closer to the original than that of the Elegies, but, on the whole, less worthy of his poetic power. It gives, however, an equally vivid account of the omens in Rome which preceded the approach of Cæsar to the city. The lines are fine, as quotation will show—

> " Fulgora fallaci micuerunt crebra sereno,
> Et varias ignis tenso dedit aere formas :
> Nunc iaculum longo, nunc sparso lumine lampas
> Emicuit caelo . . ."

Marlowe translates—

> " The flattering sky glittered in often flames,
> And sundry fiery meteors blazed in heaven
> Now spear-like long, now like a spreading torch
> Lightning in silence stole forth without clouds ".[3]

It is possible that this passage in Lucan may have suggested the speech of Calpurnia in " Julius Cæsar " and that Marlowe's version of

(1) Ovid Elegies, Bk. III, El. IX, Marlowe Trans.   (2) Ovid Elegies, Marlowe Trans.   (2) Elegies, Bk. I, El. X.   (3) Translation of Lucan, 1600, Bk. I.

" Sideris et terris mutantem regna cometem ".
" And comets that presage the fall of kingdoms "[1]

gave rise to Shakespeare's—

> " The heavens themselves blaze forth the death of
> princes ".[2]

The poems of Marlowe, and especially " Hero and
Leander ", are full of beauty and of passionate verse.
His longest work has been often and justly praised,
and yet it is only a fragment. The spirit of the love of
loveliness inspires this echo of Grecian melody, which
is " most musical, most melancholy ", musical in its
matching of sense with sound, melancholy as an
incompleted sacrifice on the altar of song. It is well
nigh impossible to say which are the most perfect
lines, but the following show Marlowe at the height
of his lyrical power. The poet describes the
innocence of girlhood—

> " a country maid
> Whose careless hair, instead of pearl t'adorn it,
> Glistered with dew, as one that seemed to scorn it,
> Her breath as fragrant as the morning rose,
> Her mind pure, and her tongue untaught to glose "[3]

the joy of the waves through which Leander swam—

> " Which mounted up, intending to have kissed him
> And fell in drops like tears because they missed him "[4]

the procession of virgins returning from the feast of
Adonis—

> " For every street, like to a firmament,
> Glistered with breathing stars, who, where they went,
> Frighted the melancholy earth, which deemed
> Eternal heaven to burn "[5]

(1) Trans. of Lucan, Bk. I.   (2) " Julius Cæsar ", Act II, Sc. 2.   (3) " Hero and
Leander ", Sest. I, 1.388.   (4) Sest. II, 1.173.   (5) Sest. I, 1.97.

and his vision of the moon : " That night-wandering pale and watery star ",[1] which finds an echo in Shelley's—

> " Art thou pale for weariness
> Of climbing heaven and gazing on the earth
> Wandering companionless "[2]

while his pictures of Hero's preparations for her lover's coming, of their meeting, and of her blushes—

> " A kind of twilight break, which through the air
> As from an orient cloud glimpsed here and there "[3]

are exquisitely painted. The night is visualised by the single line, " The air with sparks of living fire was spangled ",[4] and the world beneath the ocean in the few words—

> " Where the ground
> Was strewed with pearl, and in low coral groves,
> Sweet-singing mermaids sported with their loves ".[5]

This recalls Keats (with whom Marlowe has already been compared) in his description of the " deep-water world " where Cynthia waits Endymion—

> " On gold sand impearl'd
> With lily shells and pebbles milky white ".[6]

It is interesting to note in passing that both Marlowe and Shakespeare had the same views on the advantages of marriage, for the first writes of human beauty—

> " But this fair gem, sweet in the loss alone
> When you fleet hence, can be bequeathed to none ".[7]

(1) Sest. I, l.107. (2) Shelley, " To the Moon ". (3) " Hero and Leander ", Sest. II, l.319. (4) Sest I, l.188. (5) Sest. II, l. 161. (6) Keats, "Endymion", Bk. III. (7) Sest, I, l.245.

and the second—

> " Thy unus'd beauty must be tomb'd with thee
> Which, usèd, lives th' executor to be "[1]

but the question of their relations to each other is too large for discussion here, although Shakespeare's tribute to the " dead shepherd " must not be forgotten.[2]

The continuation of Chapman to " Hero and Leander " does not call for attention, but it may be considered as unworthy of the fragment to which it was added. It is marked by power, but by roughness of style and lack of melody, while it has little of the delicate colouring of the earlier poet. Two lyrics and a Dialogue in verse which contains none of Marlowe's genius, remain for mention. The first of these is the well-known but decidedly over-praised " Passionate Shepherd to his Love ", and the second a much more beautiful series of verses, first printed in " England's Parnassus ", with the charming opening—

> " I walked along a stream, for pureness rare,
> Brighter than sunshine, for it did acquaint
> The dullest sight with all the glorious prey
> That in the pebble-pavèd channel lay ".[3]

Although the spirit of Marlowe's work was so largely lyrical, yet his plays and poems show small variety of rhythm. His dramas are chiefly written in the unrimed pentamèter, to which he gave new power and freedom. The rush of his thought broke through the monotonous regularity of verse which had marred the translations of Surrey and the speeches of " Gorboduc ", until the language became in his hands sufficiently plastic to take the impress

(1) Shakespeare, Sonnet IV.   (2) " Hero and Leander ", Sest. I, l.176. Shakespeare, " As You Like It ", Act III, Sc. 5.   (3) " England's Parnassus ", 1600.

of his passion. For he wrote as he felt, similes, images and emotions came crowding in upon his mind to be voiced in the noble metre which later enshrined the genius of Shakespeare and Milton, with a profusion, often uncontrolled, but more often magnificent in vision and power. Poetry was the Parian marble in which he carved the joys and griefs, the aspirations and fears of a short and unprincipled life. For, although the charge of atheism brought against him by his contemporaries is probably greatly exaggerated, and seems quite incompatible with his intense love of beauty and delight in the majesty of man, yet, like so many great poets, he could not define his faith nor formulate his creed. Throughout his life his imagination over-swayed his judgment, and in a moment of passion wrecked a life of wonderful promise. The incarnation of the Eliza-bethan spirit in its love of the noble, its desire for knowledge, its too often material aims and its un-controlled passions, his death was one of the great calamities of literature, for of him, as of his "Faustus", we may say—

"Cut is the branch that might have grown full straight,
And burnèd in Apollo's laurel-bough ".[1]

Marlowe has left to his country a small but a precious gift of poetry whose beauty of expression and grandeur of thought has made him an immortal, one who has "out-soared the shadow of our night " and joined those who are " the hierophants of an unapprehended inspiration; the mirrors of the gigantic shadows which futurity casts upon the present . . . the influence which is moved not, but

(1) " Faustus ", Sc. xvi.

moves, and the unacknowledged legislators of the world ".[1] Yet his trumpet does not sing to battle, it proclaims beauty to the world, and the hearts of men echo for ever the music of his mighty line.

" Terminat hora diem, terminat auctor opus ".

(1) Shelley, " Defence of Poetry ".

A STUDY OF BROWNING'S
"PAULINE".

A Paper read before the West London Group of the English Association. October, 1923.

A STUDY OF BROWNING'S
" PAULINE ".

" Not what man sees, but what God sees—the *Ideas*
of Plato, seeds of creation lying burningly on the
Divine Hand—it is toward these that he struggles—
Not with the combination of humanity in action, but
with the primal elements of humanity he has to do;
and he digs where he stands, preferring to seek them
in his own soul as the nearest reflex of that absolute
Mind, according to the intuitions of which he desires
to perceive and speak ".[1]

In these words, which occur in his Preface to a
forged collection of Shelley letters, published in 1851,
Browning has characterised the " Subjective Poet ",
and incidentally himself. From his earliest work in
" Pauline " to the " Reverie " of " Asolando ", he
hymns the restless search of the soul of man for Truth
and the belief in some approximation to it through
the guiding force of Love. His first creation shadows
forth the essence of them all, and throughout his
poetry there is diversity of gift, but the same spirit.
The psychology gains in depth, the characterisation
grows more subtle, a philosophical speculation
mingles with the fervour of poetic insight, but the
insistence on the import and value of the human soul
is unaltered. In his balance of spiritual motive and
the resultant act, the clear vision of his mind is
revealed, for it is in this that the strength of Browning
lies—he is so splendidly certain and so gloriously
sane. " The primal elements of humanity ", the

(1) Browning Society Papers, No. 1. 1881.

inward and divine causes of which actions are the
effect, this is the realm wherein his genius is most
unslaved and potent, and here he finds the primal
energising force to be Love. Sir Henry Jones, in his
profound psychological study of the poet, writes:
" It were almost an endless task to recount the ways
in which Browning exhibits the moralising power of
love; how it is for him the quintessence of all good-
ness, the motive and inspiring cause of every act in
the world that is completely right, and how, on that
account, it is the actual working in the man of the
ideal of all perfection ".[1] Also, it is for him the
standard by which other feelings should be judged,
the reconciler between the evil of the world and the
Divine purpose, the former being a necessary opposition to wake the incentive to strive for the latter,
and the Spirit animating all created Nature. The
theme of all Browning's poetry is, therefore, in short,
the voicing of the relation of the experience of life to
the dweller in the innermost—that is Love.

But in such a world language must always be an
inadequate form of revelation, and it is often true
that Browning was only able to hint rather than to
define his meaning: as his work became more complex he counted more and more on the mental
sympathy of his reader, and when he knew that he
was being studied by a mind in tune (if less inspired
and full of genius than his own) with his, he could
dispense with many links of expression, thus becoming difficult for those who did not follow his conception and thought. In his earliest work, however,
which can be now considered in detail, the style, if
close, is clear. There is little doubt that the best

(1) Jones, " Browning as a Philosophical and Religious Teacher ". London.
1912. Chap. VI, p. 178.

approach to the more fully developed achievement
of Browning is through the introspective and the
retrospective lines of "Pauline", an unequal but
marvellous production for an age of some twenty
years.

Before passing to the subject matter and mental
characteristics of this remarkable study in reflection;
some bibliographical facts may be mentioned. In
1833, through the kindness of a relation, Browning
was enabled to publish his first work, which appeared
anonymously with the following title: "Pauline—a
Fragment of a Confession".[1] This edition is now
rare, but the British Museum contains two copies.
The poet himself was dissatisfied with the achievement, for in one volume he wrote on the fly-leaf,
" written in pursuance of a foolish plan I forget or
have no wish to remember ",[2] and later, when he
included it in the 1868 collection of his poems,
apologised for it in these words: " The first piece
in the series (' Pauline ') I acknowledge and retain
with extreme repugnance. . . . The thing was my
earliest attempt at ' poetry always dramatic in
principle, and so many utterances of so many persons,
not mine . . . a sketch that, on reviewal, appears
not altogether wide of some hint of the characteristic
features of that particular *dramatis persona* it would
fain have reproduced; good draughtsmanship, however, and right handling were far beyond the artist
at that time ".[3] He was still of the same opinion in
1888, for he then writes: " Twenty years' endurance
of an eyesore seems more than sufficient; my faults
remain duly recorded against me, and I claim per-
mission to somewhat diminish these, so far as style is

(1) Saunders & Otley, Conduit Street, London. 1833. (2) Flyleaf of "Pauline",
1833. (3) Preface to " Pauline ", 1868.

concerned, in the present and final edition where
' Pauline ' must needs, first of my performances, con-
front the reader ".[1] It is difficult to understand why
the poet condemned this poem so strongly, for even
to his contemporary in the " Repository " the work
" had truth and life in it . . . gave us the thrill,
and laid hold of us with power, the sensation of
which has never yet failed us as a test of genius.
. . . We felt certain of Tennyson . . . we are not
less certain of the author of ' *Pauline* '[2] and up to the
present there have been many admirers of this strange
but fascinating work. . . ." An article in the " St.
James Magazine " calls attention to its neglect save
by a few, " For some unaccountable reason it seems
almost forgotten, and yet there are lines in it which
no lover of poetry would willingly let die ";[3] and
William Sharp, in his " Robert Browning ", gives
perhaps the most just modern critcism on the poem.
" Never again was Browning to write a poem with
such conceptive crudeness, never again to tread the
byways of thought so falteringly or so negligently;
but never again, perhaps, was he to show so much
over-rapturing joy in the world's loveliness, such
Bacchic abandon to the ideal beauty which the true
poet sees glowing upon the forlornest height and
brooding in the shadow-haunted hollows of the
hills ".[4]

The verse of "Pauline" can be examined from two
points of view—the technical and the imaginative;
and in the former aspect the differences between the
text of 1833 and that of 1888 are of great interest.
They take the form of definite alteration, as in this
passage which runs in the early version—

(1) 1888.   (2) W. J. Fox, Vol. 7, N.S., 1833.   (3) " St. James Mag.", Vol. 7,
1871.   (4) W. Sharp, " Browning ", London, 1890, Chap. II.

> " And thus I know this earth is not my sphere,
>   For I cannot so narrow me, but that
>   I still exceed it; In their elements
>   My love would pass my reason—but since here
>   Love must receive its objects from this earth
>   While reason will be chainless, the few truths
>   Caught from its wanderings have sufficed to quell
>   All love below;—then what must be that love
>   Which, with the object it demands, would quell
>   Reason, tho' it soared with the seraphim? "[1]

but in the latter—

> " How should this earth's life prove my only sphere?
>   Can I so narrow sense but that in life
>   Soul still exceeds it?   In their elements
>   My love outsoars my reason; but since love
>   Perforce receives its object from this earth
>   While reason wanders chainless, the few truths
>   Caught from its wanderings have sufficed to quell
>   Love chained below; then what were love, set free
>   Which, with the object it demands, would pass
>   Reason companioning the seraphim? "[2]

of change in the order of words, the line " And creatures of my own were mixed with them "[3] becoming " And with them creatures of my own were mixed ";[4] of extension when the shortened pentameter " The time which was an hour that one waits "[5] is made " The time which was an hour one fondly waits "[6] and of the omission of repeated conjunctions, as, for instance, where the 1833 edition has—

> " My theories
> Were firm, so I left them, to look upon
> Men, and their cares, and hopes, and fears, and joys ";[7]

but that of 1888—

(1) 1833, l.642.   (2) 1888, l.642.   (3) 1833, l.167.   (4) 1888, l.167.   (5) 1833, l.438.   (6) 1888, l.438.   (7) 1833, l.449.

> " My theories
> Were firm, so them I left, to look and learn
> Mankind, its cares, hopes, fears, its woes and joys ";[1]

In spite, however, of Browning's second Preface, quoted earlier, it is hardly possible to say that the corrections improve the poem, of which the metre is in both cases halting except where the imagination of the poet harmonises the expression, creating lines of unforgettable beauty. There is indeed much truth in the contention of William Sharp " in ' Pauline ', written though it was in the first flush of his genius and under the inspiring stimulus of Shelley, the reader encounters prosaic passages, decasyllabically arranged ",[2] and he quotes, for example, that beginning, " Then came a pause . . ."[3] But in those pages wherein he yields himself to the influence of his musical " Sun-treader ", there his verse rises to its full height of haunting melody—in lovely simile—

> " As Arab birds float sleeping in the wind
> O'er deserts, towers and forests . . ."[4]

> " See where the solid azure waters lie
> Made as of thickened air, and down below,
> The fern-ranks like a forest spread themselves "[5]

> " For Music . . . is as a voice
> A low voice calling fancy, as a friend,
> To the green woods in the gay summer time "[6]

in joy of Grecian morn—

> " Yet, I say, never morn broke clear as those
> On the dim clustered isles in the blue sea,
> The deep groves and white temples and wet caves".[7]

and in her legend—

(1) 1888, 1.449. (2) " Robert Browning ", Chap. II. (3) 1833, 1.350. (4) 1833, 1.485. (5) 1833, 1.800. (6) 1833, 1.371. (7) 1833, 1.336.

> " An old hunter
> Talking with gods, or a high-crested chief
> Sailing with troops of friends to Tenedos ".[1]

(an echo perhaps of Marlowe)—

> " The king
> Treading the purple calmly to his death,
> While round him, like the clouds of eve, all dusk
> The giant shades of fate, silently flitting,
> Pile the dim outline of the coming doom ".[2]

The last line but one contains a metrical device repeated in the famous description of Andromeda, namely, that the verse concludes with a dactyl and spondee (" By the dark rock and the white wave just breaking ")[3] thus adding a sense of expectancy to the image. And then, there are the glorious Nature pictures of which Stopford Brooke writes, " The descriptions of Nature in this poem are more deliberate, more for their own sake, than elsewhere in Browning's poetry ", and later, after referring to painting in " Night, and one single ridge of narrow path ".[4] " He never tried it again, but passed on to suggest the landscape by a few sharp, high-coloured words, choosing out one or two of its elements and flashing them into prominence ".[5] It is in these that the poet is akin to, yet different from, the Shelley of " Alastor ". Both have pictured the woodland glade, the abode of verdant peace. The earlier poet writes—

> " Where the embowering trees recede, and leave
> A little space of green expanse, the cove
> Is closed by meeting banks, whose yellow flowers
> For ever gaze on their own drooping eyes,
> Reflected in the crystal calm . . ."[6]

(1) 1833, 1.329. (2) 1833, 1.575. (3) 1833, 1.672. (4) 1833, 1.740. (5) " Poetry of R. Browning ", 1902. (6) " Alastor ", 1.404.

the latter—

> " See this our new retreat
> Walled in with a sloped mound of matted shrubs,
> Dark, tangled, old and green, still sloping down
> To a small pool whose waters lie asleep
> Amid the trailing boughs turned water-plants "[1]

Both were one with Nature—

> " He would linger long
> In lonesome vales, making the wild his home,
> Until the doves and squirrels would partake
> From his innocuous hand his bloodless food,
> Lured by the gentle meaning of his looks,
> And the wild antelope, that starts whene'er
> The dry leaf rustles in the brake, suspend
> Her timid steps to gaze . . ."[2]

> " I can live all the life of plants, and gaze
> Drowsily on the bees that flit and play,
> Or bare my breast for sunbeams which will kill,
> Or open in the night of sounds, to look
> For the dim stars ; I can mount with the bird
> Leaping airily his pyramid of leaves
> And twisted boughs of some tall mountain tree ";[3]

and to both came visions; Shelley saw " a veiled
maid " who " Sate near him, talking in low solemn
tones ",[4] and Browning a

> " young witch, whose blue eyes
> As she stood naked by the river springs,
> Drew down a god "[5]

yet the poetry of each is individual. The seer of
" Alastor " dwells in a world of mystically intensified
beauty ; the singer of " Pauline " in that of actual
loveliness. The one speaks of—

(1) " Pauline ", 1833, 1.757.   (2) " Alastor ", 1.98.   (3) " Pauline " 1833,
1.724.   (4) " Alastor ", 1.151.   (5) " Pauline ", 1833, 1.113.

> " Islanded seas, blue mountains, mighty streams,
>   Dim tracts and vast, robed in the lustrous gloom
>   Of leaden-coloured even, and fiery hills
>   Mingling their flames with twilight, on the verge
>   Of the remote horizon "[1]

the other cries—

> " Up for the glowing day, leave the old woods !
>   See, they part like a ruined arch; the sky !
>   Nothing but sky appears, so close the root
>   And grass of the hill-top level with the air . . .
>   The clear, dear breath of God that loveth us,
>   Where small birds reel and winds take their delight"[2]

It is the contrast between the dreamer and the realist, the vision of the mystic and the man. Browning's tribute to Shelley—

> " Sun-treader, life and light be thine for ever ! "[3]

is worthy of his own and his worshippers' genius and a high eulogy of one who, like him, " images to himself the Being whom he loves and seeks in vain for a prototype of his conception ".[4]   Herein lies the essence of both poems, the poet of Shelley is nurtured—

> " By solemn vision, and bright silver dream . . .
>   Every sight
>   And sound from the vast earth and ambient air,
>   Sent to his heart its choicest impulses . . .
>   And all of great
>   Or good, or lovely, which the sacred past
>   In truth or fable consecrates, he felt
>   And knew ",[5]

but sets out to " seek strange truths in undiscovered lands ",[6] finding at the end of his quest nothing but

(1) " Alastor ", 1.555.   (2) " Pauline ", 1833, 1.789.   (3) " Pauline ", 1833.   (4) " Alastor ", Preface.   (5) " Alastor ", 1.67.   (6) " Alastor ", 1.77.

memories and death. The thinker of " Pauline ",
however, finds his powers and sings—

> " I dreamed not of restraint, but gazed
> On all things; schemes and systems went and came,
> And I was proud (being vainest of the weak)
> In wandering o'er them, to seek out some one
> To be my own; as one should wander o'er
> The White Way for a star . . ."[1]

attaining happiness through his trust in God and
Truth as shown him by the poet of love: and is able
to write—

> " Know my last state is happy—free from doubt
> Or touch of fear. Love me and wish me well ! "[2]

This conclusion is typical of the clear sanity of
Browning who " Moving about in worlds not
realised " has no " blank misgivings " and however
he may have suffered, and there is no reason to deny
that " Pauline " is to some extent auto-psychical,
knows that in faith dwells peace.

The poem then is the story of the development of
a soul, the " confession " of the difficulties which
beset a mind seeking the light. The personality of
Pauline becomes apotheosised into a guiding spirit,
but yet does not completely lose her womanhood, and
the confusions of the work arise from the mingling of
the real and imaginary. In the prefatory quotation
from Cornelius Agrippa are the words, " Nam et ego
vobis illa non probo, sed narro ",[3] and the narration is
consistent, even if lengthened by digressions, which
are, as has been said, often the most poetical
passages. The opening address to Pauline as woman
is a confession of the poet's trust in her to sympathise
with his mental experience—

(1) " Pauline ", 1833 1.404. (2) " Pauline ", 1833, 1.1039. (3) " Pauline ",
1833, Prefat. Note.

> " Thou seest then my aimless, hopeless state,
> And, resting on some few old feelings, won
> Back by thy beauty, wouldst that I essay
> The task which was to me what now thou art;
> And why should I conceal one weakness more?"[1]

He then breaks forth into recollections—

> " Thou wilt remember one warm morn when Winter
> Crept aged from the earth, and Spring's first breath
> Blew soft from the moist hills ",[2]

and cries :

> " Thou are not more dear
> Than song was once to me ",[3]

but the joy then grasped was illusion, and in the
image of the " white swan " he attempts an analysis
of his feelings, but is cheered that he can still vision
the beauties of the past " most distinct amid the
fever and the stir of after years ".[4] Perplexed, he
turns to Shelley for guidance, and in praising him
laments his own failure in the realm of song, although
" he must sing on, fast as fancies come : Rudely, the
verse being as the mood it paints ".[5] He returns to
his analysis, " I am made up of an intensest life ",[6]
and finds he can recall or forget the " dark past " at
will; that a mind of this type must seek an end, but
that his first fresh faith has gone. He tries to reason
of these hopes and fears, touches on his delight in
" wisest ancient books; All halo-girt with fancies of
my own ",[7] and how he felt within him capacities
unrevealed. Suddenly his mind awoke, but not to
peace, mental conflict swayed him, and even when
calm returned, it was not final but the result of
music's revelation and of labour for achievement.
He had passed through the waking to the beauty in

(1) " Pauline ", 1833, l.50.   (2) l.55.   (3) l.77.   (4) l.140.   (5) l.265.
(6) l.275.   (7) l.325.

things, and his " choice fell, Not so much on a system as a man ",[1] and he thought that in discipleship to a saviour " Men were to be as Gods, and earth as heaven ",[2] and his song prophetical. Pausing for a moment he tells Pauline of this time of joy, how he allowed his mind the fascination of search, the excitement of endeavour—

> " And suddenly, without heart-wreck, I awoke
> As from a dream; I said ' 'Twas beautiful,
> Yet but a dream, and so adieu to it . . .' "[3]

and with the dream—

> " First went my hopes of perfecting mankind,
> And faith in them—then freedom in itself,
> And virtue in itself—and then my motives' ends,
> And powers and loves; and human love went last "[4]

until the poet relapsed into cynicism; and from this came mental pride and the vision of " kneeling shadows " who worshipped him as king and did his bidding in the realm of fancy[5] so that he grew confident and cried—

> " No age should come on me ere youth's hopes went,
> For I would wear myself out—like that morn
> Which wasted not a sunbeam—every joy
> I would make mine and die ".[6]

Thinking that in devotion to this purpose (and the goal is that of Faustus and Paracelsus) he could find his end, he retired into himself, trusting, in the power of his poetic creation, to move men, addressing Pauline—

> " Pauline, my sweet friend, thou dost not forget
> How this mood swayed me when thou first wert mine ",[7]

(1) " Pauline ", 1868, 1.410.   (2) 1.433, 1833.   (3) 1833, 1.455.   (4) 1833, 1.465.
(5) " Pauline ", 1833, 1.480.   (6) " Pauline ", 1833, 1.508.   (7) 1833, 1.568.

and touching once again on the self-absorption to which it led, even if glorified by the poetry of the past. But a change has taken place in his mind, he has learnt that—

> " I cannot chain my soul, it will not rest
>   In its clay prison; this most narrow sphere—
>   It has strange powers, and feelings, and desires,
>   Which I cannot account for, nor explain ",[1]

and that his intense love of pleasure is incapable of real satisfaction, so he seeks

>   " but one
>   Delight on earth, so it were wholly mine ",[2]

and this restless passion joins with the longing for knowledge which suppressed is a token of the mastery of his will. But neither of these is enough, and a higher ideal rises, until he realises that given an opportunity—

> " A time requiring youth's best energies;
>   And straight I fling age, sorrow, sickness off,
>   And I rise triumphing over my decay ".[3]

Such a crisis seems to him for a moment the reconciliation of the past and present; but further reflection shows him that

> " There's some vile juggle with my reason here;
>   I feel I but explain to my own loss
>   These impulses; they live no less the same ",[4]

and that he is under a spell woven by liberty, and love of his now imaginised Pauline. Yet he knows beneath, that this is also a mood and from his heart addresses the woman—

(1) " Pauline ", 1833, l.601.   (2) " Pauline ", 1833, l.616.   (3) 1833, l.681.
(4) " Pauline ", l.689.

> " Pauline, I could do anything—not now—
> All's fever—but when calm shall come again
> I am prepared; I have made life my own "[1]

and tells her that in imagination he has lived and can live the life of animate creation, bidding her fly with him—

> " Pauline, come with me, see how I could build
> A home for us, out of the world, in thought ".[2]

Then follows the magnificent description of this " home " through which his soul and that of his love wander, " Night, and one single ridge of narrow path ",[3] but even this beautiful world does not lift the sadness from him, because he cannot taste all joy.[4] Despair seizes him—

> " O God where does this tend—these struggling aims?
> What would I have? "

and then comes the answer—

> " The last point that I can trace is, rest beneath
> Some better essence than itself—in weakness;
> This is ' myself '—not what I think should be,
> And what is that I hunger for, but God? "[5]

At this point in the poem occurs a French footnote of some length purporting to be by " Pauline ", in which she discusses the mental attitude of the poet. This is of value as it throws much light on Browning's interpretation of his work. It suggests that the writer is not entirely clear in his conception of what has passed, but that rearrangement is impossible on account of the involutions of his mind. It continues : " Je n'en crois pas moins au grand principe de toute composition—à ce principe de Shakspeare, de

(1) " Pauline ", 1833, 1.706. (2) 1833, 1.736. (3) 1833, 1.740. (4) 1833, 1.818. (5) " Pauline, 1833, 1.826.

Raffaelle, de Beethoven, d'où il suit que la concentration des idées est due bien plus à leur conception,
qu'à leur mise en exécution . . . j'ai tout lieu de
craindre que la première de ces qualités ne soit encore
étrangère à mon ami—et je doute fort qu'un re-
doublement de travail lui fasse acquérir la seconde ".[1]
In additon she touches on the achievement of the
poet, namely, an advance from one level of thought
to another with retro-vision. Browning thus shows
he realised that description of personal mental
experience in any verse was of extreme difficulty
unless allegorically made, but the final paragraph of
this ingenious interpolation is probably the safest
clue to the true interpretation of the poem. The
remaining pages are similar in style to those which
have been mentioned. After his impassioned expression of his hunger for God, follows a prayer to Him
for revelation of Himself; then, as the light breaks,
he sees the error of his previous conceptions of love,
and repentant at having denied it in the Christ (a
wonderful passage) devotes himself to it—

" A mortal, sin's familiar friend, doth here
　Avow that he will give all earth's reward,
　But to believe and humbly teach the faith
　In suffering and poverty and shame,
　Only believing he is not unloved ".[2]

Then the analysis approaches conclusion, the poetical
thinker becomes the disciple of love, which he
apostrophises in a " Pauline spiritual and actual ";
once again he returns to the past darkness, but only
to contrast it with the present peace, in which the
radiance of trust shines over him. Trust, no longer
in his own powers, but in the human and mental

(1) " Pauline ", 1833, l.819. Note by Pauline. (2) " Pauline ", 1833, l.863.

sympathy of Pauline, who loved him thought-tossed
and self-tortured, and with whom he can now pass
beyond the veil of life in transcendent vision of a
world where he knows—

> " I shall again go o'er the tracts of thought
> As one who has a right, and I shall live
> With poets, calmer, purer still each time,
> And beauteous shapes will come to me again,
> And unknown secrets will be trusted me
> Which were not mine when wavering; but now
> I shall be priest and prophet as of old ".[1]

Not unguided will he wander for the poet he worshipped will lead him—

> " Sun-treader, I believe in God and truth
> And love; and as one just escaped from death
> Would bind himself in bands of friends to feel
> He lives indeed, so, I would lean on thee.
> Thou must be ever with me, most in gloom
> When such shall come—but chiefly when I die,
> For I seem dying, as one going in the dark
> To fight a giant—and live thou for ever,
> And be to all what thou hast been to me—
> All in whom this wakes pleasant thoughts of me,
> Know my last state is happy—free from doubt
> Or touch of fear. Love me and wish me well ".

This interpretation of " Pauline ", inadequate and
mistaken as it may well be, will serve to confirm the
words " He had the courage of his aims in art, and
while he frequently shaped in verse the vigorous
movement of life . . . he went on quietly, amid the
silence of the world, to paint also the slowly inter-
woven and complex pattern of the inner life of men ".[2]

(1) " Pauline ", 1833, 1.1020, et seq. References are usually to 1833 edition
of poem. (2) " The Poetry of Robert Browning ", by Stopford Brooke; London;
1902; Chap. I, p.9.

And this first poem is a "complex pattern of the inner life ", an endeavour to explain the wakening of a soul to the revelation of the truth. If, according to modern psycho-analysis, the relief of a suppressed grief is its re-creation in the mind of the sufferer, then in "Pauline" Browning has relieved himself of the doubts and perplexities which assailed his growing manhood; for, outwardly peaceful as was his life, no one could have achieved his clear, sane optimism untried by battle with and victory over indifference and despair. There is a statement of Aristotle which may well be applied to this poet and to his "Pauline "; the philosopher is writing of Art and expresses the view that its use "is temporary emancipation from the control of certain passions by means of their excitation and subsequent subsidence ".[1] Many minds discover that they have passed through the same experiences as the lover of Pauline, and can find in his search for light a similarity to their own. To these this early creation of Browning's genius will always be a revelation and joy, nor will they perhaps fail to sympathise with the moods of the poet or to guess his meaning. Confused though it be, unequal in style, rising to glorious poetry, sinking to prosaic passage, it remains a unique study of deep passion, of mental development, and of spiritual attainment.

> "For this song shall remain to tell for ever
> That when I lost all hope of such a change,
> Suddenly Beauty rose on me again ".[2]

(1) Aristotle, " Politica ", VIII, 7.   (2) " Pauline ", 1833, l.1012.

ROBERT BROWNING'S "DRAMATIC LYRICS".

A Paper read to the West London Group of the English Association.   March, 1923.

" Bells and Pomegranates ", Numbers 3 and 7.   1842, 1845.

" Dramatic Romances and Lyrics ", 1849.

BROWNING AND HIS
"DRAMATIC LYRICS".

BROWNING in his "advertisement" to the third
volume of "Bells and Pomegranates", published in
1842, has given his own interpretation of the seemingly contradictory title, "Dramatic Lyrics" writing:
"Such Poems as the following come properly
enough, I suppose, under the head of "Dramatic
Pieces", being, though for the most part Lyric
in expression, always Dramatic in principle, and so
many utterances of so many imaginary persons, not
mine". This assumption, which he re-stated in the
two volume edition of his poems (1849) at the
beginning of the collection there called "Dramatic
Romances and Lyrics", may be carefully considered
as it will probably throw light on the poet and his
compositions. The first confusion arises from his use
of the phrase "Lyric in expression". If the essence
of lyric poetry be perfection of form and melody,
Browning is mistaken in his employment of the term,
for in few of these poems is the metre faultless or the
line and stanza well balanced. It would appear that
he interpreted the word to imply freedom of treatment and escape from a definite structure, for his
poetry is held together by thought rather than by
technical skill. This lack of verse-craft and harmony
is surprising in one of such musical appreciation.
Another characteristic of the lyric, which is absent
from much of this volume, is brevity; for a collection
which includes the fifteen sections of "In a Gondola",

the blank verse of " Artemis Prologuizes ", and the
story of " Waring ", cannot be said to be really
lyrical in spirit. The question of what importance
Browning attached to the phrase " always Dramatic
in principle " is easier to answer. To this poet drama
was not so much the interplay of event with event
but of mind with mind, and therefore the setting of
the dialogue or the analysis was of less worth than
the mental states of the participants. It is for this
reason probably that he leaves the scenery of his
poetry so much to the imagination of his reader, and
concentrates his powers to weigh the motives behind
a certain action. In spite of his claim that the poems
are the " utterances of so many imaginary persons,
not mine ", he is always thinking through the characters of his creation and, unlike Shakespeare, does
not allow external circumstances to produce an
unexpected effect. He is a careful artist and keeps
close in touch with his subject, fearing, it would
seem, to let it stand alone. When Shakespeare re-
created Falstaff he intended to subordinate him to
the story of Henry IV, but he made him so human
and natural that the knight dominates the drama,
and the author was forced to establish the dignity
of the Court, at the last moment, by his dismissal.
He risked an unjust ending for the sake of a character,
and has not spoilt his play. Browning, however,
would not have taken the risk. None of his
" dramatis personæ " are permitted to interfere with
the story on account of their too intense individuality
—their creator was concerned with a presentment of
the argument and would not allow irrelevance. This
hatred of the unnecessary to the analysis is the chief
cause of the poet's obscurity, for in his anxiety to
be cogent he omits too much, with the result that

the reader is left with many unanswered questions. All these characteristics are shown in this early collection of Browning's shorter poems, the volume which he called " Dramatic Romances and Lyrics " in the 1849 edition of his work. Before, however, examples are given some further bibliographical details must be quoted.

Of the sixteen poems comprising the third number of " Bells and Pomegranates "[1] two—entitled in this number " Madhouse Cells " I and II, but in the edition of 1849 " Johannes Agricola in Meditation " and " Porphyria's Lover "—were reprinted from the " Monthly Repository " of 1836. Of the twenty-two included in the seventh number of " Bells and Pomegranates "[2] six were reprinted from " Hood's Magazine ",[3] called in the 1849 edition " The Laboratory ", " Claret and Tokay ", " Garden Fancies ", " The Boy and the Angel ", " The Tomb at St. Praxed's ", and " The Flight of the Duchess ". The remainder were printed for the first time in these numbers. The other six volumes of " Bells and Pomegranates " contained " Pippa Passes ",[4] " King Victor and King Charles ",[5] " The Return of the Druses ",[6] " A Blot in the 'Scutcheon ",[7] " Colombe's Birthday ",[8] " Luria " and " A Soul's Tragedy ".[9] Previous to these Browning had published " Pauline ",[10] " Paracelsus ",[11] " Strafford ",[12] and " Sordello ",[13]. The two volume edition of 1849 contains the whole eight numbers of " Bells and Pomegranates " with the addition of " Paracelsus ", combining the third and seventh into one, under the title " Dramatic Romances and Lyrics ". It is this first collection of the shorter poems in this edition that

(1) " Dramatic Lyrics ", 1842.   (2) " Dramatic Romances and Lyrics ", 1845.
(3) 1844-45.   (4) I, 1841.   (5) II, 1842.   (6) IV, 1843.   (7) V, 1843.
(8) VI, 1844.   (9) VIII, 1846.   (10) 1833.   (11) 1835.   (12) 1837.   (13) 1840.

will be now considered in greater detail, for the poems grouped under the head "Dramatic Lyrics" in later compilations of the poet's works (as, for instance, that of 1887) are drawn from the "Men and Women" as well as from the volumes mentioned above.

That Browning was not satisfied with the text of the volumes of 1842 and 1845, is shown by the alterations made in that of 1849. They appear to have been introduced to improve the metre, and may be summarised under three heads : additions, inversions, and substitutions. An example of each may be given. Five lines are added in the sixth section of "Waring", the 1842 edition running—

> " He splashes, as none splashed before
>   Since great Caldara Polidore;
>   Then down he creeps and out he steals
>   Only when the night conceals
>   His face— "

but that of 1849—

> " He splashes, as none splashed before
>   Since great Caldara Polidore;
>   Or Music means this land of ours
>   Some favor yet, to pity won
>   By Purcell from his Rosy Bowers—
>   ' Give me my so long promised son,
>   Let Waring end what I begun ! '
>   Then down he creeps and out he steals . . ."

The closing four lines of " Cristina ", in the 1842 edition, are—

> " That just holds out the proving
>   Our powers, alone and blended—
>   And then, come next life quickly !
>   This life will have been ended "

but have been lengthened thus in 1849 to balance those before—

> " Life will just hold out the proving
> Both our powers, alone and blended—
> And then, come the next life quickly !
> This world's use will have been ended "

and phrases have been introduced into the irregular couplets of " Rudel to the Lady of Tripoli ". An instance of inversion is shown in " Artemis Prologuizes ", the line " So, in the blindness of his wrath exiled ", of the 1842 edition, being changed to " So, exiled in the blindness of his wrath ". Substitutions are less common than the above alterations, but one of importance may be quoted. The fourth stanza of " The Lost Mistress ", in the 1845 copy, is—

> " For tho' no glance of the eyes so black,
> But I keep with heart's endeavour,—
> If you only wish the snowdrops back,
> That shall stay in my soul for ever ".

in the 1849—

> " For each glance of that eye so bright and black,
> Though I keep with heart's endeavour,—
> Your voice, when you wish the snowdrops back,
> Though it stays in my soul for ever ! "

The poet, however, has not succeeded in obtaining true lyric melody, even by these changes, for this poem is not metrically consistent. The regular form of stanza would be a quatrain of alternate ten and eight syllable lines, but the second of the third verse has seven and the first of the last nine syllables. The same form of irregularity may be noticed in " Garden Fancies " where the lines should be of nine syllables but in fact fluctuate from eight to ten. These examples will be sufficient to prove the statement made earlier in this study that " in few of these poems is the metre faultless or the line and stanza well balanced ". Browning could indeed keep the beats of his verse symmetrical, and has done so in the couplets of " My Last Duchess " and the sexains of " The Confessional ", but he prefers the loose rhythm of " In a Gondola ". Another peculiarity which often robs his verse of smoothness is his use of forced double-rimes. They are frequent in " The Flight of the Duchess " as, for instance—

" Blesseder he who nobly sunk ' ohs '
And ' ahs ' while he tugged on his grandsire's trunkhose"

where they may perhaps be excused on the speaker's account, but may be found in other poems as in—

" Sire ", I replied, " joys prove cloudlets;
   Men are the merest Ixions— "
Here the King whistled aloud—" Let's
   Heigho—go look at our lions ",

from " The Glove ". Enough has been said to prove that Browning was careless of the technicalities of verse-form, and often guilty of harsh lines and elliptical constructions. These faults prevent his poems in this volume from fulfilling his statement that they are " for the most part lyric in expression ". Only two perhaps can be really accepted as such, the " Song "—

" Nay but you who do not love her,
   Is she not pure gold my mistress?
Holds earth aught—speak truth—above her?
   Aught like this tress, see, and this tress?
   And this last fairest tress of all,
   So fair, see, ere I let it fall "[1]

(1) 1849.

(where the double-rime may be forgiven), and " Meeting at Night", which succeeds in conveying an intense impression in twelve lines free from obscurity and inversion.

It is now time to consider how far this volume fulfils the author's statement that the poems included are " always dramatic in principle, and so many utterances of so many imaginary persons, not mine ". It has been mentioned earlier that Browning's method of dramatic presentation was " the interplay of mind with mind " and a concentration upon motive. This is clearly displayed in these pieces, of which some may be analysed in more detail. The volume of 1842 opens with the " Cavalier Tunes ", which are followed by the poems under the title " Italy and France ", I. " Italy ",[1] II. " France ".[2] The first begins "That's my last Duchess painted on the wall", and gives an example of the poet's method when he describes events from the point of view of a participant remembering them. The story is not in fact told by the Duke, but implied, and the lines—

> " Sir, 'twas not
> Her husband's presence only, called that spot
> Of joy into the Duchess' cheek : perhaps
> Frà Pandolf chanced to say— "

give an indication of what occurred, which is confirmed by the phrase—

> " She had
> A heart . . . how shall I say ? . . . too soon made glad "

and the account closes with the words (" Then) I gave commands "—

" Then all smiles stopped together. There she stands ".

(1) 1849, " My Last Duchess ". (2) 1849, " Count Gismond ".

133

But it may be deduced from the character of the narrator, shown in the remark, " and I chuse, never to stoop ", and by his placing the dowry before the bride in his contemplation of his next marriage, that the Duchess had some provocation. These are but a few of the impressions given to the reader, and the poem is one of the finest examples of Browning's power to suppress the irrelevant and imply the details necessary to the picture by suggestion. The second poem gives the chivalrous atmosphere of a tournament, and is a narrative of her justification by her champion Gismond, told by one lady to a friend. It is less remarkable than the preceding, but contains the fine lines—

> " The lie was dead
> And damned, and truth stood up instead "

and throws interesting light on the belief in " ordeal by battle ". These are followed by two poems of a different type called, in the edition of 1842, " Camp and Cloister ", I. " Camp ",[1] II. " Cloister ".[2] The first is a simple story of an incident in the Napoleonic wars, told for once in the third and not the first person, and showing few of the writer's characteristics. The second, however, is a powerful study of hypocrisy and bitter sarcasm. It is difficult to deduce the exact cause of the speaker's hatred of Brother Lawrence; unless he had been wronged by him in the world or was, as Mrs Orr suggests, acutely jealous. The extraordinary mixture of language and mental attitude in the last four lines may be quoted—

> " Blasted lay that rose-acacia
> We're so proud of ! *Hy, Zy, Hine* . . .
> 'St, there's Vespers ! *Plena gratia*
> *Ave, Virgo !* Gr-r-r- you swine ! "

(1) 1849, " Incident of the French Camp ". (2) 1849, " Soliloquy of the Spanish Cloister ".

184

"In a Gondola", which is given next in the third
volume of "Bells and Pomegranates", concludes
with a passionate tragedy, to which the reader is led
up by lines of mingled joy and fear. The incidents
are simple—the flight of two lovers by night in a
gondola from the vengeance of three Venetians and
their capture. Yet the poet has created a poem of
some length, his object probably being to produce
sympathy with the fugitives and to express the fervour of their love. Many of the verses are very striking, and the dialogue gains power from its simplicity.
The lover is more confident than his beloved, and his
petition—

> "Say after me . . .
>   This woman's heart, and soul, and brain,
>   Are mine as much as this gold chain
>   She bids me wear . . ."

is met by—

>   "Kiss me as if you entered gay
>   My heart at some noonday".

Later he visions the attack of the "Three", but
takes refuge in his love—"I reel . . . and . . . is it
Thee I feel!" Then, lest the crisis should be too
sudden, her reflections are given and his description
of their return home. Finally, they reach the steps
and the tragedy occurs, introduced by the passionate

>   "Heart to heart,
> And lips to lips! Once ere we part
> Make me thine as mine thou art!
> (*He is surprised and stabbed*)
> It was to be so, Sweet,—and best
> Comes 'neath thine eyes, and on thy breast.
> Still kiss me! Care not for the cowards! Care
> Only to put aside thy beauteous hair
> My blood will hurt . . ."[1]

(1) Text of 1842.

185

ROBERT BROWNING'S "DRAMATIC LYRICS"

This conclusion has the brevity and restraint of the highest type of dramatic art, and a whole life's tenderness is summed in the lover's anxiety about his beloved's hair. Browning, in this poem, has succeeded in vivifying his characters, but, as has been said earlier, their actions and their attitudes to each other have been thought out before the poem was written, and the story carefully balanced. This Venetian drama is followed by the " Artemis Prologuizes ", which shows the poet's method of re-telling a classical story. The description of the wreck of the chariot driven by Hippolutos is vivid, but the poem does not reveal Browning the analyst. In "Waring", which succeeds, the poet is weaving fanciful images round a friend (Mr Alfred Domett ?). The subject of the easily flowing couplets is clearly painted, and the reader feels, especially in the early part of the poem, a personal knowledge of the man who

" paced this London
With no work done, but great works undone ".

The two poems given in the Dramatic Lyrics[1] under the title of " Queen Worship " are of a different kind. The first, called " Rudel to the Lady of Tripoli ", is a lament by a troubadour who wears a sunflower as a symbol of his love, and concludes with an address to a pilgrim who is about to travel to the land of his heart's desire—

" But, as the flower's concern is not for these
But solely for the sun, so men applaud
In vain this Rudel, he not looking here
But to the East—the East ! Go, say this, Pilgrim dear"

The second is a powerful study of the sudden awakening into love of a man and woman, for the former a

(1) 1842.

136

life-long remembrance, for the latter a transient excitement. The paradox is clearly stated in the last verse—

> " Such am I : the secret's mine now !
> She has lost me—I have gained her !
> Her soul's mine : and, thus, grown perfect
> I shall pass my life's remainder . . ."

This poem contains also the fine stanza—

> " Oh, we're sunk enough here, God knows !
> But not quite so sunk that moments,
> Sure tho' seldom, are denied us,
> When the spirit's true endowments
> Stand plain out from its false ones,
> And apprise it if pursuing
> The right way or the wrong way,
> To its triumph or undoing ".[1]

The experience here expressed has been often felt, but Browning has summarised it with skill and penetration.

The two poems called in the edition of 1842 " Madhouse Cells "[2] are in some ways the most remarkable in the volume. The first is a subtle study of egotistic religious ecstasy, put into the mouth of the sixteenth century reformer. The speaker will contend that he is apart from humanity and therefore specially chosen by heaven, and at the same time affirm his ignorance of the Deity ; he will cry—

> " For as I lie, smiled on, full fed
> By unexhausted power to bless,
> I gaze below on Hell's fierce bed", and yet say—

> " God, whom I praise ; how could I praise
> If such as I might understand ".

(1) 1842 Edition. (2) 1849, " Johannes Agricola in Meditation ". " Porphyria's Lover ".

Browning's conception of "Johannes Agricola" shows the poet's skill in the interpretation of mixed motive in a single mind. The second is perhaps even more remarkable. The actual facts of the story of "Porphyria's Lover" are sordid, being the strangling of a woman by a man who fears that her love may alter; but, as handled by the poet, they become powerful, pathetic, and intensely dramatic. At the beginning he creates an atmosphere of storm and contrasts with it the warmth of the cottage to which Porphyria comes; he suggests the tumult in the woman's heart and her decision to visit "one so pale for love of her"; her subtle appeal to him by her beauty, surrender and confession; and then he gives an insight into the mind of the lover when he makes him say—

> "Be sure I looked up at her eyes
> Proud, very proud, at last I knew
> Porphyria worshipped me . . ."

Then the pride and the fear that she may fail him grow stronger, and he tells how

> "That moment she was mine, mine, fair,
> Perfectly pure and good : I found
> A thing to do, and all her hair
> In one long yellow string I wound
> Three times her little throat around
> And strangled her ",

but remorse follows passion, and in the lines—

> "No pain felt she
> I am quite sure she felt no pain "

we see its birth, gradually the silence changes it to fear, and the drama ends with the simple but unforgettable phrase—

> " And thus we sit together now,
>   And all night long we have not stirred,
>   And yet God has not said a word ! "

It is a triumph of compression and tragedy, and once again shows Browning's power of motive analysis, for although it is told in the first person the reader can follow the workings of Porphyria's mind and see the incident from two points of view. The remaining poems in the third volume of " Bells and Pomegranates " are the rapid lines " Through the Metidja to Abd-el-Kadr " and " The Pied Piper of Hamelin ". Neither of these show Browning at his best. The motion in the first is well given by the short metre and the repeated " As I ride, as I ride ", and the story in the second told with simplicity and humour, but it is to the seventh number of " Bells and Pomegranates " that attention must be turned. This volume was published in 1845 under the title of " Dramatic Romances and Lyrics ". It opens with the account of " How they brought the good news from Ghent to Aix ", a narrative poem with the same sense of movement as " Through the Metidja ", but continues with the " Pictor Ignotus ", which deserves some notice. It is, like so many of Browning's most thoughtful poems, cast in the form of a monologue, and gives the mixture of self-confidence and admiration for others which is sometimes found in the unrecognised artist. After describing the work he could have done under encouragement, he comforts himself with his frescoes in the cloisters and ends his reflections with an unanswered question—

" So die, my pictures; surely, gently die !
    Oh, youth, men praise so—holds their praise its worth ?
    Blown harshly, keeps the trump its golden cry ?
    Tastes sweet the water with such specks of earth ? "

It is a composition which reveals the poet's love and knowledge of art, but leaves in the mind the impression of finding comfort in the inevitable. It is the voicing of a mood which is well known to the sensitive spirit. The couplets which follow this soliloquy are of an entirely different atmosphere. Called in the 1845 edition "Italy in England "[1] they describe the vivid reflections of an Italian who, on a past occasion, helped to save his country. The story of his flight, the aid he received from a village woman, and his departure from her, are simply told; the lines work up to his longing to see her once more and close—

> " So much for idle wishing—how
> It steals the time ! To business now ! "

The style is clear, but as is his custom the poet breaks straight into his narrative, " That second time they hunted me ", and the events connected with, but not absolutely included by, the adventures, have to be imagined from suggestions in the lines. " England in Italy "[2] is a poem full of atmosphere, and a description of the " Scirocco " is given by the account of the doings of the peasants. It is an example of the poet's method of presentment, of creating the impression of a thing by portraying its effect. In succession to this in the 1845 edition, is placed " The Lost Leader ", a poem which has perhaps been over-explained. Whether or not it refer to Wordsworth, it is the expression of sincere, noble regret, and gains much force from the cogency of its style. It is of interest also because the poet is speaking for once in his own person, and not through the mouth of an historical or imaginary character. Before passing on, an

(1) 1849, " The Italian in England ". (2) 1849, " The Englishman in Italy ".

important difference between the text of " Bells and Pomegranates "[1] and that of the two volumes of 1849 must be noticed. The last line but three in the first copy runs " Strike our face hard ere we shatter his own ", but in the second version " Aim at our heart ere we pierce through his own ". " The Lost Leader" is followed by " The Lost Mistress ", a masterpiece of compressed passion, wherein every word has significance; the theme is somewhat similar to that of Drayton's fine sonnet, " Since there's no help, come let us kiss and part ", but whereas the earlier poet continues—

> " And when we meet at any time again,
>   Be it not seen in either of our brows
>   That we one jot of former love retain "

Browning throws a greater strain upon the lovers—

> " Yet I will but say what mere friends say
>   Or only a thought stronger;
> I will hold your hand but as long as all may
>   Or so very little longer "

and thus makes the separation more tragic. The three groups of lines called " Home Thoughts from Abroad "[2] need not be considered in detail. The first is the well known " Oh, to be in England ", the second some verses in praise of Nelson (later included in the works under the title " Nationality in Drinks "), and the third the fine passage opening " Nobly Cape Saint Vincent to the north-west dies away " and ending in the 1845 edition " Yonder while Jove's planet rises silent over Africa ", but in that of 1849, " While Jove's planet rises yonder, silent over Africa ". These are followed by the lines on " The Tomb at St. Praxed's ",[3] dated by Browning " Rome

(1) 1845.   (2) 1845.   (3) 1849, " The Bishop orders his tomb in St. Praxed's Church ".

15— ". This is another study of religious egotism, and may be compared with " Johannes Agricola ", but whereas this latter has reverence for the Deity the bishop is entirely concerned for his earthly fame and is determined to out-do his fellow ecclesiastic " Gandolf " in the splendour of his monument; and yet, and here is Browning's skill in motive analysis revealed once more, the dying man is fully aware that his " sons " will take from him all that they can get and not carry out his wishes. The mingling of these feelings is the spirit of the poem, which gives a vivid image of the hypocrisy of the time. The " Garden Fancies ", which are placed next to this, are a complete contrast. The first is a simple love-poem, wherein the lover wanders in the garden hallowed by memories but finds it less lovely than of yore—" Roses, you are not so fair after all ". The second reveals the poet as a humourist, showing the anger and literary feeling of the author in conflict over a wearisome work of some old scholastic. It is remarkable for the cleverness of its rimes and its delicate satire. Both this and the preceding poem have lines descriptive of Nature, which, although a minor note, is not absent from the poetry of Browning. Power of re-creating the passions of the past fill the quatrains of " France "[1] and the verses of " Spain ".[2] The first is in the poet's indirect method of construction and brings before the reader the intensity of jealousy seeking means of vengeance. The fascinated interest of the visitor to the laboratory in the preparation of the poison, and the way in which the wrong done is hinted but not actually stated, add to the vividness of the painting which had probably real counterparts during the age in

(1) 1849, " The Laboratory ".   (2) 1849, " The Confessional ".

which it is placed. The incidents of the second poem
are also possible under the reign of the "Inquisition",
and the vehement denunciation by the tortured
woman of Priests, Pope and Saints is tragically great.
Browning perhaps has allowed the horror of this
story to be rather too emphatic for the restraint of
the highest art, but it shows his power of suggestion
in a marvellous way. What a picture is given by the
lines—

> " A girl that laughed in beauty's pride
>   Like lilies in your world outside "

and by—

> " The horrible black scaffold drest—
>   The stapled block . . . God sink the rest ".

The terror of the fifteenth lives once more in the
nineteenth century. " The Flight of the Duchess "
is a poem of too great length for detailed consideration in this place, but its characteristics may be
mentioned. The originality of the writer is shown by
his putting the story into the mouth, not of Duke
nor Duchess, but of their retainer. This enables him
to give a view more or less dispassionate of the incidents and persons. The introduction of the magic
element by the Gipsy and her strange lyrical incanta-
tion over the Duchess, lend a touch of fancy to the
tale, and the whole romance is set in the background
of the narrator's mind and his shrewd if uneducated
remarks and comments. It is a striking re-cast of an
old legend. The Fragments given under the title
" Earth's Immortalities ",[1] are marked by simplicity

---

(1) 1849, I. " Fame "; II. " Love ".

of expression and meaning, the second having the lyric note. These are followed by the "Song", mentioned earlier in this study, "Nay but you, who do not love her", and by the couplets of "The Boy and the Angel". This imaginative story is simply told with no insistence on the suggested moral or interpretation, and shows that Browning could, if he wished, rest from his analysis of motive and character. The same intellectual rest can be seen in the lines of "Meeting at Night" and "Parting at Morning", but in neither is there any lack of concentration or of thought. Here is added in the edition of 1845, but omitted in that of 1849, the poem "Claret and Tokay", which is not worthy of Browning's skill. It is followed, however, by one of the poet's most powerful creations, the haunting lines of "Saul". This poem is not complete in the seventh volume of "Bells and Pomegranates", nor in that of 1849. It was first given in its full text in the collection entitled "Men and Women" (1855). Just as the "Pictor Ignotus" and the "Tomb of St. Praxed" show the author's interest in art, so this sustained and noble work proves his belief in the appeal of music. The conception of the silent, solitary and suffering king in the darkened tent gradually re-wakened to life by the songs of David, is a remarkable expansion of the beautiful words—

"And it came to pass, when the evil spirit from God was upon Saul, that David took an harp and played with his hand; so Saul was refreshed".

Nor is the language unworthy of the theme; many lines are vividly pictorial as—

" And first I saw nought but the blackness; but soon
 I descried
 A something more black than the blackness; the vast,
  the upright
 Main-prop which sustains the pavilion—and slow into
  sight
 Grew a figure, gigantic, against it, and blackest of all—
 Then a sunbeam, that burst thro' the tent-roof—
  showed Saul ".

others are full of ecstasy as—

" And the wild joys of living; the leaping from rock up
 to rock—
 The rending their boughs from the palm-trees, the
  cool silver shock
 Of a plunge in the pool's living water ".

The poem indeed is yet another proof of Browning's
gift of historical imagination, and his capacity to
present to the reader a vision of the past. It seems
a pity that the poet was not content to close his
volume with this great example of his genius. It is,
however, followed by two poems, the first the couplets
called " Time's Revenges ", and the second " The
Glove ". The former is the confession, cast in monologue, of a poet for whom a friend has the greatest
affection but who holds this gift lightly in comparison with his own devotion to a lady, although fully
aware that she would forget him if she should find
a more enthralling interest. The description of his
passion is compressed into a few striking lines—

  " To think, I kill for her, at least
   Body and soul and peace and fame,
   Alike youth's end and manhood's aim,
   As all my genius, all my learning,
   Leave me where there's no returning ".

(The last couplet is omitted in the edition of 1849.)

It is a clever but complex example of the poet's study of mixed motive in a single mind. The last poem of the collection tells the story of " The Glove and the Lion ", which had been treated simply by Leigh Hunt in his stanzas opening " King Francis was a hearty king and lov'd a royal sport " through the mouth of the poet Ronsard. The incidents are not, therefore, directly described as in the earlier poem, but form a background to the conversation of the King and the speaker. Browning was not content to leave the crisis of the tale with the words—

> " Your heart's queen, you dethrone her?
> So should I . . . 'twas mere vanity
> Not love set the task to humanity ",

but saw an opportunity for analysis and continues the poem as a dialogue between the poet and the lady, wherein the latter explains how she had so long been forced to take the assertions of De Lorges for deeds, that she wished to put them to the test. Finally, Ronsard relates how she marries a youth who offered to serve her when she was disgraced, and concludes—

> " Venienti occurrite morbo
> With which moral I drop my theorbo ".

This completes the seventh number of " Bells and Pomegranates " and the " Dramatic Romances and Lyrics " of 1849. It is now possible to emphasise the chief characteristics shown by Browning in these poems and to compare them with his own definition of them : "Such Poems as the following come properly enough, I suppose, under the head of " Dramatic Pieces " being, though for the most part lyric in expression, always dramatic in principle, and so many utterances of so many imaginary persons, not mine ". It has been pointed out above that the term " Lyric " is used in error, unless we accept the view that it implies freedom of form, and that Browning is a careless metrist. The main principles behind his work, however, have also been stated. These are : concentration on the analysis of either simple or complex motive, control over the mind and action of his created personalities, closeness of touch with his subject and avoidance of irrelevant details. In addition to these which may be seen in the background of the whole collection of verse, are the following talents which are prominent in certain poems : power in suggestion of tragedy, as in " My Last Duchess "; of atmosphere, as in " Porphyria's Lover "; and of environment, as in " The Englishman in Italy "; power of creating an impression by describing its effect, as in " Christina "; skill in the compressed portrayal of passion, as in " The Lost Mistress " and " In a Gondola "; and in the use of historical imagination to recall a past event or interest, as in " The Flight of the Duchess " or the " Tomb at St. Praxed "; effective handling of horror, as in the " Confessional "; and of paradox, as in " Time's Revenges "; love of beauty in art, as in " Pictor Ignotus "; and faith in the healing power of music, as in " Saul "; and lastly, but in a less degree, an appreciation of Nature. These are some of the characteristics of this great poet, and surely they are almost entirely those connected with the dramatic principle.

The creations of Browning are the imaginations of his own mind projected through that of " so many imaginary persons ". In their interest and intensity, their vividness and variety, they are all children of one parent—a thinker, a poet, and a dramatist. For the whole body of Browning's work proves his possession of this triple endowment. It is found in growth in "Pauline", mature in "Paracelsus", and unwithered in "Asolando"; it is the completed circle and the crown of his genius.

DIRECT APPEAL IN ENGLISH POETRY.

A Paper read before the " Fortnightly Society " of Hampstead. February, 1923.

DIRECT APPEAL IN ENGLISH POETRY.

IT is not necessary in the consideration of this subject to quote definitions of poetry. It will suffice if the significance attached by the writer to the words " direct appeal " be explained and emphasised. He would interpret them as follows—" Direct appeal in poetry is the result of a capacity possessed by a poet to realise the essential beauty of the worlds of Nature and of Thought, and to reveal them briefly but clearly to man ". This statement is open to criticism and discussion, but an endeavour will be made to establish its truth. The first question that arises is whether there be any difference between " direct " and " indirect " appeal. This may be answered by the realisation that poetry impresses itself upon the mind in two ways; either by a series of cumulative images of beauty, or by the sudden formulation of a universal truth, and that while the former is a gradual process, the latter has the swiftness of intuition. The first may be considered as " indirect ", the second as " direct " in its effect. The perception of the lovely in an imaginative world, whether it be derived from the contemplation of Nature, or through mystical ecstasy, is a gift independent of learning, and while capable of training, cannot be created in those who have not its germ. The faculty of instantly perceiving a great ideal, however, depends largely on the receptivity of a mind, whose capacity may be developed by study and practice. The former, or

" indirect " power is a primal necessity in poetry as poetry, but of less importance in the world of men than the latter, or " direct " power which will raise the forethought of every-day to a higher value. True poetry cannot be divorced from beauty, but neither can noble action from thought. The result of this affirmation is that while the mind of the seer will appeal directly to those of his own priesthood who worship the same loveliness, it will be out of touch with the world at large, and that although the poet with the capacity to express a great truth will probably be less acutely sensitive to the subtleties of imagination, he will reveal a new incentive to men in direct and simple phrase. The definition given above has been worded so as to allow for both forms of appeal, the purely poetical and the intuitively practical, but only if both are " direct ". Examples may make these points clearer. A poet, in a few lines, gives, to a mind in tune with his, a sharply drawn mental picture of some natural beauty; the appeal to the second imagination is "direct". Another poet, seeking to describe some lovely scene, builds up his landscape, detail by detail, until the completed creation is the sum of various carefully considered parts, the beauty of the whole depending on the skill of the cumulative composition. This is the "indirect" appeal in the realm of poetry and is outside the scope of this study. A writer, in some brief but finely phrased verse, expresses a thought which has occurred to the many but has hitherto been unstated. This is the " direct " appeal. A second writer decides to instruct mankind through the medium of a didactic poem, thus employing the method of " indirect " appeal. Both forms of expression are the function of poetry, but that of simple and clear statement

the greater. It is this that may now be considered,
as manifested in the works of some of the English
poets.

There are among the thirteenth century lyrics many
lines which give in simple and " direct " language,
images of beauty. Such are, for instance, these—

> " Lenten ys come with love to toune,
>   With blosmen ant with briddes roune,
>   That al this blisse bryngeth;
> Dayes-eyes in this dales,
> Notes suete of nyghtegales,
>   Uch foul song singeth.
> The threstelcoc him threteth oo,
> A-way is huere wynter wo,
>   When woderove springeth;
> This foules singeth ferly fele,
> Ant wlyteth on huere wynter wele,
>   That al the wode ryngeth ".[1]

Here is a fresh and unsophisticated appeal to the
loveliness of Spring, which gives to the reader the
same spontaneous feeling of joy that it must have
produced on the mind of the writer. Nor was the
more human note neglected. There is tragedy in
these lines—

> " For hire love y carke ant care,
> For hire love y droupne ant dare,
> For hire love my blisse is bare
>   Ant al ich waxe won,
> For hire love in slep y slake,
> For hire love al nyht ich wake,
> For hire love mournynge y make
>   More then eny mon.
> Blou northerne wynd!
> Send thou me my suetyng ",[2]

(1) Oxford Book of English Verse, 1918, No. 3.   (2) Oxford Book of English
Verse, No. 4, st. 5.

which give an immediate impression of sorrow. Even
the short effective monitory lines of the poet who is
concerned for the welfare of man may be found in
the " Proverbs of Hendyng ", composed probably in
this century. These contain good advice—

> " Such lores ase thou lernest,
> After that thou sist and herest,
> Mon, in thyne youthe,
> Shule the on elde folewe ".[1]

The work of Langland, Gower and Chaucer may
now be mentioned, and considered in regard to
" direct appeal ". The " Vision of Piers Plowman ",
although it contains no simple nature description,
has passages which give a vivid picture and which
help us to realise the life of the lower orders of
society in the fourteenth century. The characters,
it is true, are allegorical, but the painting of the
scene is from direct observation. A good example
is furnished by the account of " Glotoun " and his
adventures in the Ale-house, to which he has been
enticed by " Beton, the brewestere ". His departure
is vividly described—

> " There was laughyng and louryng and ' let go the
>   cuppe ',
> And seten so til euensonge and songen umwhile,
> Tyl glotoun had y-globbed a galoun an a Iille . . .
> He myghte neither steppe ne stonde er he his staffe
>   hadde;
> And thanne gan he go . . .
> Somme tyme aside and somme tyme arrere . . .
> And whan he drowgh to the dore thanne dymned his
>   eighen,

(1) " Specimens of Early English " (R. Morris), p. 97.

He stumbled on the thresshewolde an threwe to
the erthe.
Clement the cobelere caught hym bi the myddel,
For to lifte hym alofte and leyde him on his
knowes ".[1]

In the work of Gower, however, the note of " direct
appeal " is absent, and his long tales of advice drawn
from Ovid and other sources are typical of the Court
school which was dependent on allegory and convention. The same lack may be noticed in the early
and minor work of Chaucer, although there is
simplicity and direct self-revelation in the Prologue
to the " Legend of Good Women " where the poet
writes—

" And, as for me, though that my wit be lyte,
    On bokes for to rede I me delyte,
    And in myn herte have hem in reverence,
    And to hem yeve swich lust and swich credence,
    That ther is wel unethe game noon
    That from my bokes make me to goon,
    But hit be other upon the haly-day
    Or elles in the joly tyme of May ".[2]

In the " Prologue " to " The Canterbury Tales ",
however, we return to pictures of fourteenth century
life. It is not necessary to quote the many shrewd
criticisms made by the writer on his fellow-travellers,
but only to observe the intense realism of their contrasted characters. Because their peculiarities
appealed " directly " to Chaucer he was able to make
them appeal " directly " to us, and in this capacity
lies his genius. His power of succinct imagery and
simile is not, however, limited to the " Prologue " of
his great work; scattered among the various tales

(1) " Piers the Plowman ", passus 5, ll.344-354. (2) Chaucer, " Legend of
Good Women ", Prol. A, l.29.

are lines that appeal directly to the heart. Such are,
for instance—

> " Have ye nat seyn som tyme a pale face,
> Among a prees, of him that hath be lad
> Toward his deeth, wher-as him gat no grace,
> And swich a colour in his face hath had,
> Men mighte knowe his face, that was bistad,
> Amonges all the faces in that route . . ."[1]

the description of the assassin—" The smyler with
the knyf under the cloke ",[2] and the sorrowful words
of Arcite—

> " What is this world? What asketh men to have?
> Now with his love, now in his colde grave
> Allone, with-outen any companye ",[3]

while mother-love speaks in the prayer of Grisild—

> " That, but my lord forbad yow, atte leste
> Burieth this litel body in som place
> That bestes ne no briddes it to-race ".[4]

The note of Nature worship is not frequent in
Chaucer, although his love of the Spring was probably
more genuine than that of the average Court-poet of
his day, but his appeal is rather to the emotions, for
he possesses pathos without sentimentality, and
humour without bitterness. The merit of " direct
appeal " is not altogether absent from the work of
his Scottish followers, although it is not found in the
English, Lydgate, Occleve, Skelton and Hawes. The
vigorous realism of Dunbar, in such verses as the
" Daunce in the Queenis Chalmer ", gives us a vivid,
if unpleasant picture of a fifteenth century Court-
revel ; and the touch of a poet on whom Nature made

(1) " Canterbury Tales ", " Man of Lawe ", l.645. (2) and (3) " Canterbury
Tales ", " Knightes Tale ", l.1999, 2777. (4) " Canterbury Tales ", " Clerkes
Tale ", l.570.

a clear impression is seen in some of the Prologues to the translation of the "Aeneid" by Gavin Douglas. It shows in his lines describing a Scotch Winter—

> " Reveris ran reid on spait with wattir broune,
>   And burnis hurlis all thair banks adoun;
>   The grund stude barrand, widderit, dosk and gray,
>   Herbis, flouris and gersis wallowit away,
>   Woddis, forestes, wyth naked bewis blout
>   Stud strypit of their weyd in every hout ",[1]

which are refreshing after the many conventional passages on the Spring that abound in the poems of this period. It is, however, among the unknown poets of the time that some of the most " direct appeal " is found. Who was the author of the exquisite simile in a song to the Virgin—

> " He came al so still
>   There his mother was,
>   As dew in April
>   That falleth on the grass "[2]

or of the passionate quatrain—

> " O western wind, when wilt thou blow
>   That the small rain down can rain?
>   Christ, that my love were in my arms
>   And I in my bed again !"[3]

We can only say that their writers possessed the capacity to realise an essential beauty and to reveal it briefly but clearly to man.

Early sixteenth century verse in the hands of Wiat, Surrey, and their followers, is strangely " indirect "; there are few natural similes and little intensely expressed feeling, although Wiat on one occasion

(1) Gavin Douglas. Prol. to Bk. VII., Trans. of " Aeneid ". (2) and (3) Oxford Book of English Verse, Numbers 23 and 27.

achieves the line " The howgy okes have rored in the wynd ",[1] and on another the sincere little lyric beginning—" Forget not yet the tryed intent ", while Surrey has this quatrain—

> " Spyte drave me into Borias raigne,
> Where hory frostes the frutes do byte,
> When hilles were spred and every playne
> With stormy winters mantle whyte ".[2]

but neither poet can match the simple sincerity of the anonymous—

> " My heart is high above, my body is full of bliss,
> For I am set in luve as well as I would wiss ",[3]

probably contemporaneous with their work. The mention of Wiat raises a point which has not as yet been considered, namely, whether " Satires " be a form of " direct appeal ". They often contain, it is true, compressed wisdom and epigrammatic reflection; but is there not an artificiality of tone in a poem written with the object of criticising some error or abuse, which must of necessity rob it of the instantaneous conception which is the mark of the most clearly inspired poetry? The writer would submit that verse of this nature is beyond the scope of this study on account of its " indirect appeal ". Surely it is true to say that more spirits have been thrilled by a moment's vision of beauty or of truth (for such is the " direct appeal " in poetry, according to the arguments quoted earlier in this paper) than by judgments possibly biased, or admonitions systematically applied. We may therefore leave satiric, as we have left gnomic poetry, outside these pages.

(1) Wiat, " Poems ", " Resounde ye wodes ". (2) Surrey, " Poems ", " Syns Fortune's Wrath ". (3) Oxford Book of English Verse, No. 52.

DIRECT APPEAL IN ENGLISH POETRY.

In the consideration of the early sixteenth century we were struck by the lack of " direct appeal " in the chief poets of the period; in the latter decades we are impressed by its scope, but at the same time interested to observe that poetry is forming two schools, one which interprets life by poetry, the other, poetry by life; the former, following our definition, we may class as " indirect ", the second as " direct ". Both divisions have their recognised leaders; Sydney and Spenser head the one class, Shakespeare and the dramatists the other. It will be well perhaps to enlarge this last statement. Sydney, no less than his greater friend, was a " poet's poet ". Little guidance for practical life can be deduced from the " Arcadia " or from the " Astrophel and Stella "; far less indeed than from the "Faery Queen", which, although allegorical in scheme and romantic in expression, is inspired with a noble idealism and faith in the virtues of man. It is not that the conception underlying the great Epic of Faeryland is not of direct interest to humanity, but that its treatment by a ceaseless succession of beautiful images and pictures distracts the attention from the original aim of the poet " to pourtraict . . . the image of a brave knight, perfected in the twelve morall virtues ".[1] In the later books indeed Spenser himself appears to have forgotten his purpose and allows his verse to flow on with little justification for its creation save an intense joy in beauty, which, although it be " its own excuse for being ", is a cause of perplexity to the reader who looks for a single guiding beam instead of a prismatic radiance. The " remoteness " of this poet has been emphasised for his work has perhaps the most " indirect appeal " in our literature, and yet in its

(1) Spenser, " Faery Queen ", Intro,

own realm is difficult to surpass. The atmosphere of Spenser's world is lovely and pure, but is too rare to be breathed with ease and delight by those unaccustomed to it, and to such he can never appeal. It is a vivid contrast to turn from " walking through woods of legend to the music of romance " to the work of Shakespeare and his fellow-dramatists. We descend from a world of aetherial poetry to an interpretation of life in words which " come home to Mens Businesse and Bosomes ". Just as it has been impossible, owing to lack of space, to quote examples to prove the " indirect appeal " of Spenser's verse, so it is not possible to give instances of the marvellous skill possessed by Shakespeare to express the essence of a beauty, a feeling or a thought. Innumerable lines and passages will spring to the mind where a vivid picture flashes on the eye, whether it be the heralds of the Spring—

> " daffodils
> That come before the swallow dares, and take
> The winds of March with beauty ",[1]

the repose of death—" After life's fitful fever he sleeps well ",[2] or the realisation of the brevity of life—

> " We are such stuff
> As dreams are made on, and our little life
> Is rounded with a sleep "[3]

he voices our thoughts for us and becomes our mouthpiece in the deeper moments of life. He is indeed the poet of " direct appeal " to the heart of man. It was the same, but in a lesser degree, with the other Elizabethan dramatists, who often make an impression at once simple, immediate and profound. Owing

(1) Shakespeare, " Winter's Tale ", Act IV, Sc. 3. (2) " Macbeth ", Act III, Sc. 2. (3) " Tempest ", Act IV, Sc. 1.

to the number of poets who flourished at the end of the sixteenth century, it has been found necessary to concentrate attention, and that only inadequately, on the leaders of the two schools of verse which then arose. In the remainder of the time at our disposal it will but be possible to mention the chief poets of the last three hundred years and to suggest to which division they belong.

Passing on, therefore, to Milton we may place him among the writers of "indirect appeal; for just as Spenser dwelt in an imaginative world of colour and romance, so he was at his greatest in a visionary realm of power and rebellion. Sir Walter Raleigh was wise when he wrote, "There are no children in any of Milton's poems. . . . None of the edifying speeches (in 'Paradise Lost') could have been made in the presence of such an auditor, or such a critic ".[1] Have we not here another standard of judgment, and does not this fact justify the inclusion of Spenser and Milton among the poets whose interpretation of life was poetical rather than practical? Dryden, who was primarily a satirist, and Pope, in spite of the moral reflections in his "Essay on Man", are outside the scope of this paper. Gray was academic, and Thomson a poet of cumulative description more than of direct interpretation in the world of Nature; Collins, it is true, in his "Ode to Evening", and Blake in some of his songs, displayed a more simple treatment of beauty and imagination; but in the seventeenth and eighteenth centuries, as in the fifteenth, it is to the lesser lyrical writers that we must go for "direct appeal". The Elizabethan and Jacobean Anthologies, the Caroline singers, and the many half-forgotten verses of the "age of reason"

(1) Walter Raleigh, "Milton", Chap. III.

will furnish examples of simplicity, freshness and charm. Space does not permit quotation of specimens in proof of this, but the opening lines of four lovely lyrics may perhaps be given. There is the anonymous " Madrigal ", " My love in her attire doth show her wit ".[1] There are the day-spring verses of D'Avenant, " The lark now leaves his wat'ry nest ";[2] the pathetic stanzas of Wither, " How near me came the hand of Death "[3] and Logan's " To the Cuckoo ", " Hail beauteous stranger of the grove ",[4] with innumerable others by Herrick, Herbert, Campion, and their followers, which express some beauty or thought briefly but clearly to man. Before the poets of the nineteenth century are considered, mention must be made of two writers who, while containing passages of " direct appeal ", indulged in poems of some length in their efforts to give a picture of contemporary life and thought. The realism of Crabbe is marked by a meticulous love of detail, the imagination of Cowper by a strange limitation of outlook. It is difficult to decide in which division they should be placed, but on account of this lack of succinctness and universality, it may be wise to class them among the poets of " indirect appeal ". A digression must be allowed in this paragraph to estimate the claim of the Ballad to belong to the poetry of instant impression. Many of these verses have the qualities of motion, vivid description and pathos; they are usually brief and their metres short. If it be seldom that they finely express a thought their incidents hardly ever fail to remain in the mind of the reader, and surely this is due to their " direct appeal ".

(1) Oxford Book of English Verse, No. 63.   (2) Oxford Book of English Verse, No. 301.   (3) Oxford Book of English Verse, No. 239.   (4) Oxford Book of English Verse, No. 476.

DIRECT APPEAL IN ENGLISH POETRY.

The poets of the nineteenth century are so numerous, and cover so many branches and aspects of life and of imagination that it is quite impossible to consider even the greatest among them without danger of misjudgment. A sincere attempt, however, to estimate their poetry on the lines of our definition cannot be either fruitless nor beyond the subject of this paper. Space will only permit reference to the chief names of the period, to Wordsworth, Coleridge, Shelley, Keats, Byron, Tennyson, Browning, Arnold and Swinburne, and in the work of each writer it should not be forgotten that the tendency of the century was towards the combination of " direct and indirect appeal ".

This tendency is revealed in the poetry of Wordsworth, which falls into two divisions. There are the poems of insight into the emotions and into the wonders of Nature, lyrics, stanzas and lines of truth, freshness and simplicity ; and also the long egotistical moralisings which, however interesting as showing the growth of a mind, have little appeal to the heart. The former or " direct " note in Wordsworth places him high among the interpreters of beauty, the latter or " indirect " composition among the poets of cumulative effect. If we consider the first in its clarity to express the real genius of this writer, he is truly a creator of instant impression. In Coleridge, on the other hand, the reflective dream is more important than the actual event, and he belongs almost entirely to the world of poetic imagination and to the poets whose appeal is remote from humanity. The " direct " touch is even more absent from his work than from that of Shelley, who was keenly alive to the sufferings of his fellow-men and interpreted for them the ideal of freedom in terms of the

ideal of love. Yet it is not possible to class the latter
seer with those whose lines have dwelt in the memory
of man after a single reading. Keats, the poet, is
akin to Spenser in his worship of ideal beauty and
truth; but in Keats, the man, as shown by his letters,
we have pregnant reflections on practical life. It is
in the first aspect that he must be considered in this
connection, and while we place him among the
singers of "indirect appeal" these lines in
"Hyperion"—

> "O folly! for to bear all naked truths,
> And to envisage circumstance, all calm,
> That is the top of sovereignty"[1]

occur to us to prove us wrong. Judging, however,
on the whole body of his poetry we are right in calling him a "poet's poet". As a contrast to the work
of Keats we may take that of his contemporary
Byron, whose popularity with his age is sufficient
proof of his "direct appeal" to it, an appeal which
although less strong to-day can still make itself felt
in many unforgettable lines such as, "Who would be
free, themselves must strike the blow".[2]

This quotation is given by Courthope as an
example of "the hereditary national quality of condensing thought in an epigrammatic form",[3] and this
characteristic is certainly marked in those poets who
have been classed as writers of "direct appeal"; it
is also covered by our definition. Tennyson rarely
showed this power of succinct expression. He is a
poet of subtle charm and magic, yet in spite of his
beauty of language and interest in the problems of his
time, he seldom crystalises the result of his thought
into brief and memorable form, for in comparison

(1) "Hyperion", Bk. II.   (2) Childe Harold, Cant. II, St. lxxvi.   (3)
Courthope, "Life in Poetry, Law in Taste", 1901, p. 298.

with the quantity of his work, he has few great single lines. Although his genius, knowledge and inspiration made him the leader of a school of poetry, his influence with the many was rather due to his position than to their belief that in him they could find the expression of their feelings, and for this reason and on account of the architectural quality of his verse, we may place him among the poets of "indirect appeal". In contrast to Tennyson, whose effects and creations are built up into a perfect whole, may be considered Browning, who cared less for the expression than for the reality of his thought. If the lack of instant impression in the former were due to his cumulative method of composition, the want of "direct appeal" to his age in the latter was the result of his rapidity of conception and carelessness of form. In reality, and it is being proved to-day, Browning was a poet whose works are filled with a noble, optimistic, and tersely expressed philosophy of life, and as such, is far more than his technically perfect contemporary, a poet of "direct appeal". If the standard of Courthope, mentioned above, be applied to him, numerous "epigrammatic truths" will be found scattered, nay, crowded in his poetry. The verdict of the present has reversed the judgment of the previous century, and Browning is now discovered to contain more guidance for man than Tennyson, who was then considered the great revealer of truth. Matthew Arnold, in many respects a nineteenth century Gray, is a poet remote from the multitude, and touches real life but seldom. Pure and cold, his style and thought have a beauty which is appreciated by the poet, but which removes him from humanity. He is, like Coleridge, a writer of "indirect appeal". The same may be said of Swinburne whose subjects are beyond the scope of ordinary life, and who is little concerned with his fellow-men: but no poet has pleaded more " directly " for a recognition of the glory of the sea, and it is difficult to read his poems on the ocean without a feeling of space and of freedom. From the point of view of our definition, however, he must be placed in the same class as Arnold, Coleridge, and many of our great poets. If reference be made to the preceding pages we find in this division—Gower, Wiat, Surrey, Spenser, Sydney, Milton, Gray, Thomson, Crabbe, Cowper, Shelley, Keats, Tennyson, and the three writers of " indirect appeal " mentioned above. As a balance to this on the side of " direct appeal " are the early English Lyrics, Langland, Chaucer, Shakespeare, the Dramatists, the Anthologists, the Ballad-writers, Wordsworth, Byron, and Browning.

The poets of the first group depend for their influence and appreciation upon an imagination alive to poetry, while those of the second appeal instantly to the mind seeking for guidance in life. If the possession of the former apprehension be a higher gift than practical insight, then the writers who receive it are of greater value to the world than those to whom it is denied; if it be not so, then the poets of " direct appeal " render a truer service to mankind. Keats has suggested a solution to both hypotheses—" I think poetry should surprise by a fine excess, and not by singularity; it should strike the reader as a wording of his own highest thoughts, and appear almost a remembrance ".[1] In the use of the words " fine excess " he justifies the attitude and creation of purely imaginative poetry; in the belief that " it should strike the reader as a wording of his

(1) Keats. Letters, Feb. 27th, 1818.

own highest thoughts " he stresses, in the writer's
opinion, the need for poetry to interpret practical
life as well as a world of vision, and to express for
man a clear call to endeavour and achievement. It
is this incentive to progress, this " direct appeal "
to reality, that has made the influence of Shakespeare, and poets of his type, so powerful over the
minds of men. Poetry in their work becomes a
guardian-angel over humanity, an angel because it
is divine in its origin, a guardian since it can protect
them from the dangers on their way. Poetry may
be able—

> " To see a world in a grain of sand,
>   And a heaven in a wild flower;
> Hold infinity in the palm of your hand,
>   And eternity in an hour ",[1]

but it cannot thus attain the end for which it was
created; it cannot fail to do so when it becomes a
guide to—

> " Strengthen the wavering line,
>   Stablish, continue our march,
>   On, to the bound of the waste,
>   On, to the City of God ".[2]

.   .   .   .

It is not possible to consider here the question of
" direct appeal " in contemporary poetry, as this
is too close to be judged in its proper perspective;
it may be noted, however, that whereas some modern
poets have broken away from tradition in order to
gain realism, others are still following out the old
and established rules of composition. Which school

(1) Blake, " Auguries of Innocence ".   (2) Arnold, " Rugby Chapel ".

will be of the greater advantage of man it is at present difficult to say. Poetry, like all art, must progress, but history proves than no advance can be independent of the past, and that development is achieved not by iconoclasm but by adaptation. It is now time to conclude this study of a subject which is capable of more detailed treatment and fuller discussion. The writer is aware that his definition and divisions may be thought to be arbitrary and his estimate erroneous. He is convinced, however, that " direct appeal " is the primal necessity of the poetry which is to live in the heart and mind of a people, and that the greatest poets are those who are the most in touch with humanity.

PERSONAL ELEGY IN ENGLISH POETRY.

"Ave atque Vale".

A Lecture given at Hampstead. February, 1924.
Sir Israel Gollancz in the Chair.

PERSONAL ELEGY IN ENGLISH POETRY.

In English Literature the chief forms of poetic creation have, like poetry itself, eluded definition—probably because they are suggestive rather than concrete. The impression made on the mind by the words lyric, drama, epic or elegy, for example, is different, but in an attempt to determine their exact scope there is difficulty, for each is found to merge into the other; the epic can be dramatic, the drama lyrical, the lyric an elegy. How, therefore, can one form be treated independently? Only if the writer be allowed to make for himself certain rules and standards of judgment, arbitrary perhaps, but necessary to compress the subject within reasonable limits. Nor need this limitation be dangerous to the function of critcism, or mistaken in application, if the unity of poetry be not forgotten.

Guided by these reflections, the consideration of the English elegy may be approached, and at the outset a problem of definition arises. The word is derived, as are most of our poetic terms, from the Greek; but in that language the noun " *elegos* " means firstly a mournful poem, and then by reduction, a poem in the elegiac metre or couplets of hexameter and pentameter, thus nearing the kindred " *elegeion* " by which this verse-form was known, and from which the adjective " *elegeiakos* " was deduced.[1] In English, however, the earlier use of

(1) " Liddell and Scott " Greek-English Lexicon, 8th edition.

" *elegos* " prevailed, and the adjective " elegiac ", technically referring to metre only, obtained the general significanc of mournful, due, no doubt, to the fact that in our poetry there is no recognised verse-form for use in poems of this type, as they are concepts rather than moulds.

The title " elegy ", therefore, may, by definition, be applied to any poem of which the spirit is mournful or pensive, but not of necessity to verse in memory of the dead, although it is most usual in this association. General reflections on the brevity of life, laments for disappointed love or departed happiness, all may come under this term, but need not be dealt with here, for even if it be possible to claim the designation " personal elegy " for these; it is permissible to limit it to the particular form which voices the affection and admiration for lost friend or hero. The thoughts of a poet on his own existence and achievement are of necessity personal, but are also subjective; while the song of tribute to the dead, although no less personal, is objective. It is, therefore with " personal elegy " in its objective sense that the following pages will deal, touching, albeit inadequately, on some of the great gifts of song laid by poets on the tomb of promise or fulfilment, not on the brief statement of the epitaph, but on the deeply-thought elegy of affectionate remembrance and undying hope. For finish of execution is not enough in poetry unless it be joined to sincerity of feeling and restraint of passion—while in elegiac verse genuineness of emotion is essential. This is the quality by which the greatness of " personal elegy " must be judged, and it is a note clearly struck by our greatest elegists; not a mere catalogue of merits in the dead, not an opportunity for the author to show

PERSONAL ELEGY IN ENGLISH POETRY.

his skill in construction or extravagance in grief, but a cry from the heart tuned to sound a responsive chord in the heart of the reader.

It is a sign of the richness of English poetry that, ever since the time of Chaucer, no age has been without its elegy on beloved or heroic character. At the beginning of the fourteenth century there is the anonymous lament over the death of Edward the First[1] which would appear to be a translation, in the same metre, from a French poem of earlier date.[2] The writer is evidently in earnest, but allies himself with the popular feeling, bidding his fellow-countrymen " wring their hands for the prize of Christendom ". In the same century, but towards its close, are two poems which really mark the beginning of true English elegiac verse, " The Book of the Duchesse "[3] by Chaucer, and " Pearl "[4] by an unknown poet. The first is Chaucer's tribute to the memory of " Blaunche ", first wife of his patron, John of Gaunt. It is a poem of considerable length, following the style of the time in construction. The wearied poet falls asleep over a " romaunce " of " Ceyx and Halcyone ",[5] dreams that he sees " a black knight " (John of Gaunt ?) bewailing his loss under a tree, and then wakes as a castle bell strikes twelve, with his book still in his hand. The spirit of the poem is that of the " Romaunce of the Rose " which was painted, in his vision, round the poet's room, and the description of the beauty and virtue of " Blaunche " is given in a detail which is wearisome. Nor has Chaucer succeeded in making the desolate lover a really pathetic figure, although his lines—

(1) 1307. (2) " Political Songs of England "; Ed. T. Wright; Camden Soc., London, 1839. (3) 1369 (Skeat). (4) 1370? (Gollancz). (5) Ovid, Metam: XI, l.410; Ed. Teubner; Vol. II.

173

" I have of sorwe so greet woon,
That joye gete I never noon,
Now that I see my lady bright,
Which I have loved with al my might,
   Is fro me deed, and is a-goon.
Allas, O Deeth, what ayleth thee,
That thou noldest have taken me,
Whan that thou toke my lady swete?
   That was so fayr, so fresh, so free,
   So good, that men may wel y-see
   Of al goodnesse she had no mete "[1]

have simplicity and directness. This lack of appeal
to the reader in the poem as a whole may be due to
the fact that the poet is expressing the emotion of
another rather than his own, for the opening wherein
he describes his difficulty in sleeping is vivid enough;
or that the metre chosen, the octosyllabic couplet,
lacks seriousness and weight; or, again, that the point
of the piece is lost in the frequency of classical
reference and lack of balance in theme-treatment. It
is not a great personal elegy, and while interesting
historically, has little appeal to the heart. The last
defect is absent from the other fourteenth century
elegy " Pearl ". The sincerity of the writer and the
bitterness of his loss, shine forth from this allegorical
yet personal lament. The poem may be studied with
the questions of its date, authorship and text, in the
edition of Sir Israel Gollancz[2] wherein his beautiful
metrical version fronts the original. It is, however,
its spirit rather than its letter which may be
emphasised here, and this is truly elegiac. The
emotion is real, the theme of the missing Pearl appear-
ing to her sorrowing father in a vision of white wonder
and bright bliss, his glimpse of the New Jerusalem,

(1) " Works of Chaucer ", Oxford Ed.; p. 88, l.475.   (2) " Pearl ", edited, with
a modern rendering etc., Sir Israel Gollancz, Litt.D., etc.; 1921.

and his petition to cross the river dividing living and
dead, is closely woven through a poem, ordered yet
free, restrained yet imaginative. Fine, however, as
are the dream-pictures, beautiful as are the descriptions—

" The marvels of that wondrous flood !
Beauteous its banks with beryl bright;
with music sweet its waters swept;
with whispering voice it wander'd on.
And in the depths shone glittering stones;
as glint through glass they glimmer'd and glow'd;
as streaming stars in the welkin shine
on a winter night, when dalesmen sleep.
Each pebble set there in that pool
was an emerald, sapphire, or goodly gem,
that all the water with light did gleam—
the glamour was so wondrous rare "[1]

there is a wonderfully human touch in the poet's
entrance into the garden at the time of the harvest
glory—

" 'twas August at a festal tide,
when corn is cut with keen-edg'd hook "[2]

ORIGINAL TEXT.

(1) " The dubbemente of tho derworth depe
Wern bonkegh bene of beryl bryght;
Swangeande swete the water con swepe,
Wyth a rownande rourde raykande aryght;
In the founce ther stonden stonegh stepe,
As glente thurgh glas that glowed & glyght,
As stremande sternegh, quen strothe-men slepe,
Staren in welkyn in wynter nyght;
    For vche a pobbel in pole ther pyght
    Watgh emerad, saffer, other gemme gente,
    That alle the loghe lemed of lyght,
    So dere watgh hit adubbement ".

(2) " In Augoste in a hygh seysoun,
    Quen corne is coruen wyth crokegh kene ".

(1) Edition cit. Stanza X.   (2) Edition cit. Stanza IV.

and in his swoon upon the grave of his beloved child—

" Before that spot my hands I clasp'd,
for care full cold that seized on me,
a senseless moan dinned in my heart,
though Reason bade me be at peace.
I plain'd my Pearl, imprison'd there,
with wayward words that fiercely fought;
though Christ Himself me comfort show'd
my wretched will worked aye in woe.
    I fell upon that flowery plat;
    such fragrance flash'd into my brain,
    I slid into a slumber-swoon
    o'er that precious Pearl without a spot ".[1]

It is indeed a poem remarkable both for its time of
composition and for its careful construction, but
especially—and herein lies the claim to remembrance
—it is a heart-song of bereavement, holding lines such
as those last quoted which have a universal appeal.
Finally, it set a standard of expression and sincerity
that the following age failed to reach.[2]

The fifteenth century was strangely poor in fine
poetry, and still poorer in " personal elegy ". There
was, it is true, the tribute of Occleve to Chaucer, with
its plaint to Death—

ORIGINAL TEXT.

(1) " Bifore that spot my honde I spenned,
    For care ful colde that to me caght;
    A deuely dele in my herte denned,
    Thagh resoun sette my seluen saght.
    I playned my perle that ther watgh penned,
    Wyth fyrce skyllegh that faste faght;
    Thagh kynde of Kryst me comfort kenned,
    My wreched wylee in wo ay wraghte.
        I felle upon that floury flaght,
        Suche odour to my hernegh schot,
        I slode vpon a slepyng-slaghte,
        On that precios perle wyth-outen spot ".

(1) Edit. cit., St. V.   (2) " A Manual of the Writings in Middle English ",
1050—1400, by J. E. Wells; London, 1916.

> " She mighte han taried hir vengeance a whyle
>   Til that som man had egal to thee be;
>   Nay, lat be that; she knew wel that this yle
>   May never man forth bringe lyk to thee,
>   And hir offyce nedes do not she;
>   God bad hir so, I truste as for the beste—
>   O maister, maister, God thy soule reste "[1]

and the lines of Gower[2] and of Lydgate[3] which are
evidently sincere—but with the exception of the
memorial verses by Skelton on King Edward the
Fourth[4] and on Henry, Earl of Northumberland[5, 6,]
and perhaps the ballad of Sir Patrick Spence "[7] there
is little that calls for notice here. The first mentioned
poems are the product of a writer whose reality of
sentiment, except in satire, may well be doubted.
The stanzas on King Edward the Fourth are written
in the person of the ruler and have small merit, while
the eulogy of Northumberland, touching on the slay-
ing of this lord, advising his son, and concluding with
a fine prayer to the Trinity, is more elegiac but lacks
earnest thought and true personal feeling.

The chief " personal elegies " of the sixteenth century group themselves around the romantic figure of
Sir Philip Sidney. But at the opening of this period
a Scotch poet, in a remarkable lament, paid tribute
to his fellow-writers. Dunbar's " Lament for the
Makaris "[8] closes with the following pathetic lines
to Death—

> " Sen he has all my brether tane,
>   He will naught lat me lif alane,
>   On force I man his neyxt pray be,
>   Timor mortis conturbat me "[9]

(1) " Gouvernail of Princes ", c. 1412, St. 301. (2) " Confession Amantis ",
Lib. 8, 1.2941; c. 1393. (3) " Fall of Princes ", Prol., St. I, 1.1; c. 1430-38.
(4) 1483. (5 and 6) 1849. " Poetical Works ", Ed. Dyce; 2 Vols, Vol. I; p. 1
and 6, 1843. (7) " Percy Reliques "; ed. Wheatley; Vol. 1, p. 98; 1891. (8) 1507.
(9) Poems of Dunbar; 3 Vols.; Early S. Text Soc.; 1893; V. 11, p. 51.

which ring true. Mention may also be made of the
eulogies by Surrey on Sir Thomas Wiat, first published in " Tottel's Miscellany ",[1] which, while sincere
in feeling are conventional in expression, the best
lines are perhaps—

" A hart, where drede was never so imprest,
   To hyde the thought, that might the trouth avance,
In neyther fortune lost, not yet represt,
   To swell in wealth, or yeld unto meschance ".[2]

In the same collection is the lament of Nicholas
Grimald upon his Mother (a forerunner of Cowper's
more famous poem) genuine in grief and affection;
and various memorial poems in the forms of epitaphs.
The most important of the verses composed in
memory of Sir Philip Sidney are those of Spenser,
whose " Astrophel "[3] laments the fate of the " gentle
shepherd " who devoted his life to his beloved Stella
in verse, courage and constancy. It is a poem with
many beautiful lines, such as—

" And many a Nymph both of the wood and brooke,
   Soone as his oaten pipe began to shrill,
Both christall wells and shadie groves forsooke,
   To heare the charmes of his enchanting skill;
And brought him presents, flowers if it were prime,
   Or mellow fruit if it were harvest time "[4]

but robbed of deep feeling by conventionality of
expression, a fault less noticeable in the succeeding
" Doleful Lay of Clorinda ".[5] Neither of these, however, nor " The Mourning Muse of Thestylis " and
" The Pastorall Aeglogue " by Lodowick Bryskett,

(1) "Songes and Sonettes"; Ed. Arber; 1870, p. 29. (2) Ditto. (3) " The
Works of Edmund Spenser"; Globe Edition; 1918; p. 559. " Astrophel ", c.
1595. (4) Spenser; Ed. cit., p. 560, St. 8. (5) Ed. cit., p. 562.

printed with them, equal this beautiful verse of
Matthew Roydon—

> " A sweet attractive kinde of grace,
> A full assurance given by lookes,
> Continuall comfort in a face,
> The lineaments of Gospell bookes;
> I trowe that countenance cannot lie
> Whose thoughts are legible in the eie "[1]

which rises in simplicity from a throng of Elizabethan
conceits. The " Epitaph " by Sir Walter Raleigh on
the " Scipio, Cicero, and Petrarch of our time " is
marked by a personal note and a restraint of imagery,
lacking in the fore-mentioned poems—

> " Nations thy wit, our mindes lay up thy love;
> Letters thy learning, thy losse, yeeres long to come;
> In worthy harts sorrow hath made thy tombe,
> Thy soule and spryght enrich the heavens above ".[2]

These do not, however, exhaust the collection of
elegies on Sidney, but space only permits reference
to one other. Spenser's " Ruines of Time "[3] is a
great elegiac poem, striking the note of the cruelty
of death in a stanza which recalls those of Villon's
pathetic " Ballade des Seigneurs du Temps Jadis "[4]
and emphasising the transience of life and the tem-
porality of power while affirming as an antithesis the
permanence of poetry. It is full of imaginative
pictures, and although too long and wayward, shows
that Spenser could, in his greatest work, rise above
the writers of his time in thought and reflection.
There is real sincerity in these lines on Robert Dudley,
Earl of Leicester, which precede the poet's reference
to Sidney—

(1) Ed. cit., p. 568, St. 18. (2) Ed. cit., p. 571, St. 11. (3) 1591, Ed. cit.
p. 489 (4) Villon Oeuvres, Ed. P. Jannet.

> " I saw him die, I saw him die, as one
>   Of the meane people, and brought foorth on beare;
>   I saw him die, and no man left to mone
>   His dolefull fate, that late him loved deare;
>   Scarse anie left to close his eylids neare;
>   Scarse anie left upon his lips to laie
>   The sacred sod, or Requiem to saie "[1]

The chief characteristics of the elegies on Sidney are, perhaps, their luxuriance of imagery and their pastoral treatment of theme; which while great qualities in poetry tend to rob the poems of that solemnity and restraint which are the mark of the most deeply-felt songs of mourning. Nor is this most sensitive chord of the human heart profoundly heard in other sixteenth century elegies. The "Daphnaida" of Spenser,[2] in memory of the Lady Douglas Howard, has stanzas such as the following—

> " Yet fell she not as one enforst to dye,
>   Ne dyde with dread and grudging discontent,
>   But as one toyld with travaile downe doth lye,
>   So lay she downe, as if to sleepe she went,
>   And closde her eyes with carelesse quietnesse;
>   The whiles soft death away her spirit hent,
>   And soule assoyld from sinfull fleshlinesse "[3]

but, as in the " Ruines of Time ", the poet speaks through the mouth of another—and the elegy is not a " personal " lament. It is, however, deserving of more recognition for its melodious verse and for the power shown in " Alcyon's " denunciation of life[4] and his pilgrimage of preparation for the coming of his love—

(1) Ed. cit., p. 491. (2) Ed. cit., p. 542, 1591. (3) " Daphnaida ", St. 37.
(4) St. 57.

" Yet, whilest I in this wretched vale doo stay,
  My wearie feete shall ever wandring be,
  That still I may be redie on my way
  When as her messenger doth come for me ;
  Ne will I rest my feete for feeblenesse ;
  Ne will I rest my limmes for frailtie,
  Nor will I rest mine eyes for heavinesse ".[1]

Before passing to the work of the other Elizabethan
Elegists, mention must be made of the eleventh
Aeglogue of the " Shepherd's Calendar "[2] written in
memory of an unknown lady " Dido ", in elaborate
stanzaic form[3] and, according to the Glosse, in imitation of " Marot, his song which he made upon the
death of Loys, the frenche Queene " ;[4] but if they be
compared, the English song misses something of the
grace of the French quatrains. The minor poets of
the sixteenth century did not produce many elegies.
Gascoigne's " Complaynt of Phylomene "[5] is one of
the earliest poems definitely entitled " An Elegye ",
but the name does not apply to this description
by the nightingale of her mythical sufferings. There
is more spirit of remembrance in the verses addressed
by Turbeville to the Earl of Surrey, paying tribute
to him—

" Whose Penne approoude what wit he had in mue,
  Where such a skill in making Sonets grue ",[6]

but both this and his " Epitaphes on Maister
Edwardes ", the musician,[7] are superficial and conventional. The " Epytaphes " of Googe[8] are no more
interesting although there is vigour in that on **M.**
Shelley, slain at Mussebroughe—

(1) " Daphnaida ", St. 66. (2) Ed. cit., p. 480, Nov. (1579). (3) 10, 10, 10,
10, 10, 7, 7, 4, 10, 4, ababbccdbd. (4) C. Marot. " Oeuvres ", Ed. P. R.
Auguis, 5 Tomes. Tom. 4, p. 67. (5) 1575. Chalmer's Eng. Poets, Vol. II,
p. 586. (6) " Epitaphes, Songes & Sonets ", 1567. (7) Vol. cit., pp. 620, 651. (8)
" Eclogues, Epitaphes & Sonettes ", Ed. Arber, 1563, p. 69, 1871.

" With charged staffe on fomyng horse his spurres with
 heels he strykes,
And forewarde ronnes with swiftye race among the mortal
 pykes,
And in this race with famous ende to do his Countrey good,
Gave onset fyrst upon his Foes and lost his vital blood "[1]

and mention in other poems of Phaer (translator of
Virgil) and of Grimald. Finally, reference must be
made to the elegies of Sylvester and Breton—the
former wrote poems in memory of Henry, Prince of
Wales, and in tribute to Sir Philip Sidney—both
artificial and unnecessary, while his panegyric of the
late wife of his friend Dr. Hill, and his verses in
memory of Lady Hellen Branch[2] although more personal are much tinged with the eulogistic style of the
time and by a lack of imagination that results in
bathetic couplets.[3] Breton is more successful in this
type of poem as his "Amoris Lachrimae"[4] on Sidney
shows. It is personal, pathetic and freer from pastoral
and classical imagery than many elegies of this time,
but it does not keep up the level of sincerity reached
in the opening stanzas. On the other hand, his
" Epitaph upon the Poet Spencer "[5]—

> " And if anie Graces lyve
> That will vertue honour gyve,
> Let them show their true affection
> In the depth of grief's perfection,
> In describing fourth her glory
> When she is most deeply sorry,
> That they all may wish to here
> Such a song and such a quier,
> As with all the woes they have,
> Follow Spencer to his graue "

(1) Ed. cit., p. 71. (2) " Lacrymae Lacrymarum ", 1613; Works, Ed. Grosart,
Edin.; 2 Vols., 1880; Vol. II, pp. 275, 279, 328. (3) 1594. (4) 1592, Works,
Ed. Grosart, Edin., 1879; 2 Vols., Vol. I. (5) " Melancholike Humours ", 1600;
Works, ed. cit., p. 24.

is flowing, but brief and shallow. This short chronicle and critcism of the sixteenth century elegy proves once more the many-sidedness of the Elizabethan age. No tribute to the dead seemed more simple and fitting than lament or eulogy, and poets, while paying their debt to friend or patron, did not forget each other. Surrey remembered Wiat; Spenser, Chaucer;[1] Breton, Sidney; and although " personal elegy " was still too often a medium for the exhibition of convention and self-advertisement, it was sometimes earnest and sincere. Both types of verse-memorial fill the years of the seventeenth century, a period made for ever rich by the " Lycidas " of Milton.

The number and variety of the " personal elegies " in the seventeenth century make it impossible to do more than touch upon some of the most important writers and their work in this form. Shakespeare is really outside the subject of this paper, but his lament in " Cymbeline "[2] should not be forgotten; but Jonson, whose poem " To the Memory of my Beloved Master William Shakespeare and what he hath left us " is a fine tribute from one poet to another; is a clear and vigorous elegist. There is the ring of sincerity and the note of real affection in the couplets—

" My Shakespeare rise, I will not lodge thee by
Chaucer or Spenser, or bid Beaumont lie
A little further to make thee a room;
Thou art a monument without a tomb,
And art alive still while thy book doth live
And we have wits to read and praise to give "[3]

of which the first three lines alude to the " Elegy " by William Basse, opening—

(1) Spenser, Ed. cit., F.Q., Bk. IV, Cant. II, st. 34. (2) " Cymbeline ", Act IV, Sc. 2, 1.258. (3) Works of Jonson, Ed. Cunningham, 3 Vols., London, 1871. " Underwoods ", 1641; Vol. 3, p. 287.

> " Renowned Spenser, lie a thought more nigh
>   To learned Chaucer, and rare Beaumont, lie
>   A little nearer Spenser, to make room
>   For Shakespeare, in your threefold, fourfold tomb "[1]

Not only Shakespeare, but others, did Jonson commemorate in his virile verse. The " Ode on the death of Sir H. Morison ",[2] the " Elegy on Lady Jane Pawlet, Marchioness of Winchester"[3] and the "Eupheme" on Lady Venetia Digby (in Ten Pieces)[4] are perhaps the most important. The first contains the well-known passage—

> " A lily of a day
>   Is fairer far, in May,
>   Although it fall and die that night
>   It was the plant and flower of light :
>   In small proportions we just beauties see,
>   And in short measures life may perfect be "[5]

while the style of Pindar, on which it is modelled, is well imitated. The second is less interesting and does not convince the reader that the emotion of the poet is sincere ; while the third is of some length— the most important section being the " Elegy on my Muse ".[6] This is marked by extravagance of imagination, although it possesses such similes as—

> " Nor can the bruised heart want eloquence ;
>   For prayer is the incense most perfumes
>   The holy altars, when it least presumes ".[7]

Jonson himself was the subject of many elegies, some of which will be considered later with the work of their authors. Two other poets who belong to the early years of the seventeenth century, and whose elegiac work is of interest, are Daniel and Drayton.

(1) Works of W. Basse, Ed. W. Bond, 1893 (1633). (2) Ed. cit., p. 342. (3) Ed. cit., p. 354. (4) Ed. cit., p. 360. (5) Jonson Ed. cit., p. 343, Vol. 3. (6) Jonson, Ed. cit., Vol. 3, p. 363. (7) p. 363.

The former has left a long poem in memory of " The Earl of Devonshire ",[1] which, after the usual opening and address to the grave,

> " Where all attendance and observance ends,
> Where all the sunshine of our favour sets,
> Where what was ill no countenance defends,
> And what was good, th' unthankful world forgets "[2]

continues to describe its hero's martial successes and finally gives his reflections on his death bed. It is marked by vigour and real desire to praise, but the poet cannot ever quite escape the conventional tricks of his period. The five " Elegies " of M. Drayton, " Upon the three Sonnes of the Lord Sheffield drowned in Humber",[3] "On Lady Penelope Clifton",[4] " On Sir Henry Raynsford of Cliford ",[5] " On Lady Olive Stanhope",[6] and "On Mistress Ellianor Fallowfield ",[7] are all conventional in style and, with the exception of that on Raynsford, devoid of personal feeling. In this poem the writer really feels the grief for his friend, which he expresses, but it is a laboured rather than a flowing composition. The following lines from the " Elegy " on Lady Clifton[8] are the best in the tribute—

> " Her delicacie, louelinesse, and grace,
> With such a Summer brauery deckt the place ;
> But now alas, it lookt forlorne and dead ;
> And where she stood, the fading leaues were shed ".[9]

In passing, reference must be made to this poet's remarkable " Epistle to Henery Reynolds, of Poets and Poesie "[10] wherein he mentions and characterises the chief singers up to his time. Neither Daniel nor

(1) 1623. (2) Ed. cit., Chalmers Poets, Vol. 3, p. 519. (3) " Minor Poems of M. Drayton ", Ed. C. Brett, Oxford, 1907, p. 97. (4) p. 102. (5) p. 113. (6) p. 116. (7) p. 121. (8) and (9) Drayton, Ed. cit., p. 103. (10) Drayton, Ed. cit., p. 108.

Drayton are really great as elegists, for in both the essence of real emotion is absent. Turning to Donne, an important seventeenth century writer, two groups of " Elegies " will be found; the first consisting of twenty love-poems,[1] which need not be considered here; the second containing more elaborate verse and entitled " Epicedes ",[2] with which may be included " The Anatomy of the World ";[3] a long production in memory of Elizabeth Drury, divided into two " Anniversaries "[4] and a " Funeral Elegy ".[5] It is a poem wherein the writer's love of subtle metaphysics exceeds his interest in the person eulogised, and the death of its subject is only a starting point for hypotheses on the future existence of the soul. These lines are, however, well-known—

> " her pure and eloquent blood
> Spoke in her cheeks, and so distinctly wrought,
> That one might almost say, her body thought ".[6]

The remainder of the poem, though often striking, is not instinct with either sincerity or with passion. The other " Obsequies " are similar in extravagance of conception and occasional vigour of expression, and there is some beauty in these lines from the " Second Elegy on Mistress Boulstred "[7]

> " The clearer soul was call'd to endless rest . . .
> And, waited on by angels, home was brought,
> To joy that it through many dangers sought.
> The key of mercy gently did unlock
> The doors 'twixt heaven and it, when life did
> knock "[8]

but the note of deep personal sorrow is absent from these works. It is a relief to turn from these long

(1) 1633-69.   (2) 1633, 35.   (3) 1611, 1612.   (4) 1611, 1612.   (5) " Poems of John Donne "; Ed. E. K. Chambers; Muses Lib.; 2 Vols.; 1896; Vol. II, p. 102. (6) Donne, Ed. cit., p. 135.   (7) Ed. cit., p. 92.   (8) Donne, Ed. cit., p. 92.

and formal elegies to the pathetic simplicity of Sir
John Beaumont in his lament for his son[1] with the
lovely lines—

" Deare Lord, receive my sonne whose winning love
  To me was like a friendship, farre above
  The course of nature, or his tender age
  Whose lookes could all my bitter griefs asswage;
  Let his pure soule, ordain'd sev'n yeeres to be
  In that fraile body, which was part of me,
  Remain my pledge in Heav'n, as sent to shew
  How to this port at ev'ry step I goe "[2]

which far surpasses his more elaborate poems on
" Lady Penelope Clifton "[3] and on " The Earle of
Southampton ".[4] Of the same beautiful sorrow as
Beaumont's remembrance of his child is the anony-
mous ballad of "Helen of Kirkconnell "[5] with haunt-
ing stanzas—

" I wish I were where Helen lies;
  Night and day on me she cries,
  O that I were where Helen lies,
    On fair Kirkconnell lea.

  Curst be the heart that thought the thought,
  And curst the hand that fired the shot,
  When in my arms burd Helen dropt,
    And died to succour me ".

Passing over the poem of Drummond on "The Death of
Sir William Alexander "[6] and the musically expressed
" Fourth Eclogue " of Browne's " Shepherd's Pipe "[7]
on Thomas Manwood, both in the conventional
pastoral style, leaving also the verses in memory of
Jonson by Ford, Cartwright, Feltham and others,[8] all

(1) and (2) Chalmers, Eng. Poets, Vol. 6, p. 40. 1629. (3) Eng. Poets, Vol. 6,
p. 41. (4) Eng. Poets, Vol. 6, p. 42; 1624. (5) The Ballad Book, Ed. W.
Allingham, 1864, p. 356. (6) Chalmers, Drummond, Vol. 5, p. 686 (1616).
(7) Chalmers, Eng. Poets, Browne, Vol. 6, p. 318 (1614). (8) Jonson, Ed.
cit., Vol. 3, p. 496 (1638).

in the strain of excessive praise, seven more elegists
of this period may be considered, namely, Cowley,
Waller, Denham, King, Marvell, Milton, and Dryden.
Cowley was the author of several memorial poems,
the most interesting being those on Vandyke, Wotton,
Wm. Hervey and Crashaw. The first is a well-com-
posed tribute, passably sincere, containing these
lines, a pattern for the true artist—

> " His all-resembling Pencil did out-pass
> The mimick imag'ry of looking-glass,
> Nor was his Life less perfect than his Art,
> Nor was his Hand less erring than his Heart "[1]

the second is over-eulogistic, endowing the subject
with an extravagant gift of tongues, and written in
a style wherein neatness of expression outweighs
depth of feeling.[2] His poems to the memory of
Hervey and Crashaw are, however, fine. The former,
more especially in the earlier verses, strikes the note
of solemn pathos and simplicity which is the essence
of " personal elegy ", while the opening stanza
creates an impression of gloom—

> " It was a dismal and a fearful night,
> Scarce could the Morn drive on th' unwilling Light,
> When Sleep, Death's Image, left my troubled breast,
>   By something liker Death possest.
> My eyes with Tears did uncommanded flow;
>   And on my Soul hung the dull weight
>   Of some Intolerable Fate.
> What bell was that? Ah, me : Too much I know ".[3]

His poem on Crashaw is less impressive, although it
describes well the character of this mystic's verse,
whose Muse—

(1) Cowley, Works, Ed. Grosart, 2 Vols., 1881, Vol. I, p. 138; Miscellanies,
1656. (2) Cowley, Ed. cit., V. I, p. 136. (3) Ed. cit., V. I, p. 141.

188

> " did well disdain
> That her Eternal Verse employ'd should be,
> On a less subject than Eternity "[1]

and it is far above that on " Katherine Philips "[2] in
emotion. It has not, however, the vigour of these
lines from an earlier elegy on the " Sonne of Sir T.
Littleton "[3] who, as his younger brother—

> " Struggled for life with the rude wave . . .
> Leapt in, and when hope no faint beam could show
> His charity shone most; ' thou shalt ', said he,
> ' Live with me, Brother, or I'le dye with thee ' ".[4]

Cowley's elegiac work is uneven, but, as has been
seen, he can rise occasionally to feeling and sincerity.
Waller was not a great elegist and has left few
memorial verses, although several epitaphs. The
lines in tribute to "Lady Rich"[5] and those on "Lady
Sedley[5] belong to the artificial style of the time, and
are marked by facile expression but little emotion;
even his poem on the " Death of Cromwell ",[6] albeit
forceful, is robbed of any real value as a " personal "
lament, by its proximity to the panegyric of
Charles.[7] The same criticism may be passed on the
work of Denham, whose elegy on " Lord Hastings "[8]
is of the conventional type, but whose poem on
Cowley[9] is of interest as expressing his views of a
contemporary writer. Henry King, whose beautiful
" Exequy "[10] is well-known, and rightly so, for it
is genuine in sorrow and emotion, has these fine
lines—

(1) Ed. cit. V. I, p. 164; Occasional Verses; 1663-8. (2) Ed. cit., V. I, p. 137;
Miscellanies; 1656. (3) Ed. cit., V. I, p. 28. (4) " Sylva ", 1636, p. 28. (5)
Waller Poems, Ed. T. Drury, 1893, p. 37, 243. (6) Ed. cit., p. 162, 1659. (7)
1660. (8) Eng. Poets, Vol. 7, p. 243, 1650. (9) Eng. Poets, Vol. 7, p. 247. (10)
Poems of H. King, Ed. L. Mason, 1914 p. 51.

> " Sleep on my Love in thy cold bed
> Never to be disquieted,
> My last good-night. Thou wilt not wake
> Till I thy fate shall overtake,
> Till age, or grief, or sickness must
> Marry my body to that dust
> It so much loves, and fill the room
> My heart keeps empty in thy Tomb "[1]

but it is hard to select for quotation as the poem should be read as a whole. It is strange that the author of this " personal " lament, and of these lines on his children—

> " Though their dayes are few
> They scarcely sinne, but never sorrow knew,
> So that they might well boast they carry'd hence,
> What riper ages lose, their innocence "[2]

could write the conventionally eulogistic elegies on " The Incomparable Charls the First "[3] and on " The Victorious King of Sweeden "[4] while those on " Lady Rich " and " Lady Stanhope "[5] justify his lines in the overstrained poem on Donne—

> " At common graves we have Poetick eyes,
> Can melt themselves in easie elegies;
> Each quill can drop his tributary verse,
> And pin it with the Hatchments, to the Herse ".[6]

His verses on Jonson and Prince Henry[7] are no more remarkable. King is indeed a fertile but unequal elegist, whose flowing couplets are but occasionally weighed with deep feeling. Marvell has left but one elegy which need be considered here, although his lines on Charles in his famous " Horatian Ode "[8]—

(1) Poems, Ed. cit., p. 54, 1664. (2) Ed. cit., p. 57, 1664. (3) Ed. cit., pp. 137, 159, 1648-49. (4) Ed. cit., p. 89. (5) Ed. cit., pp. 75, 121. (6) Ed. cit., p. 87. (7) Ed. cit., pp. 81, 83. (8) Marvell, Miscellaneous Poems; Nonesuch Ed.; London; 1923.

> " He nothing common did or mean
> Upon that memorable Scene;
>   But with his keener eye;
>   The Axes edge did try :
> Nor call'd the Gods with vulgar spight
> To vindicate his helpless Right,
>   But bow'd his comely Head
>   Down as upon a bed "[1]

should not be forgotten : this is the " Poem on the
Death of O. C. ".[2] It is a long elaborate eulogy of
Cromwell's virtues and a too favourable estimate of
his character, containing some lines of remarkable
power—

> " Oh humaine glory, vaine, oh death, oh, wings,
> Oh worthlesse world; oh transitory things;
> Yet dwelt the greatnesse in his shape decay'd
> That still, though dead, greater than death he lay'd
> And in his alter'd face you something faigne,
> That threatens death; he yet will live againe ",[3]

but is too much influenced by the fact that it is a
" state " rather than a " personal " lament. With
the " Lycidas " of Milton, a famous poem and the
subject of much criticism, is reached. The facts connected with its composition are well known. In 1637
his college friend, Edward King, was drowned, and
Milton wrote his lament in the same year, although
it was not published until 1638, when it appeared
with elegies by other admirers. The poem is pastoral
in form and therefore hampered by the conventions
associated with this type of verse. The greatness of
the monody lies in the skill with which the poet has
handled his medium and succeeded in making his expression hauntingly melodious. The lines are flowing,
but the imagery perhaps over-crowded; for there is

(1) Ed. cit., p. 116, 1681.   (2) Poems, Ed. cit., p. 140, 1681.   (3) Ed. cit., p. 146.

a lack of fitness in the introduction of St. Peter's denunciation of the Church in Milton's day; while the call to the Muses, Nymphs and River Gods, although in keeping with the manner of the poem, lends an artificiality to an elegy of which the opening stanza is both personally felt and affectionately sincere. The wonderful address to the Valleys to

> " Purple all the ground with vernal flowers.
> Bring the rathe primrose that forsaken dies,
> The tufted crow-toe and pale jessamine,
> The white pink, and the pansy freakt with jet,
> The glowing violet . . .
> Bid amaranthus åll his beauty shed
> And daffadillies fill their cups with tears,
> To strew the laureate herse where Lycid lies "[1]

is a beautiful nature tapestry, but is surpassed by the simplicity of " While the still Morn went out with sandals grey ".[2] " Lycidas " had a lovely wreath of memorial verse, as did Milton's other and perhaps closer friend, Charles Diodate in the poet's " Epitaphium Damonis ",[3] but there is a different note in the early poem " On the Death of a Fair Infant ",[4] a less studied verse, and to some, a more personal emotion—

> " O fairest flower, no sooner blown but blasted,
> Soft silken primrose fading timelessly,
> Summer's chief honour, if thou hadst out-lasted
> Bleak Winter's force that made thy blossom dry;
> For he being amorous on that lovely dye
> That did thy cheek envermeil, thought to kiss,
> But kill'd alas, and then bewail'd his fatal bliss ".[5]

Space does not permit more than a reference to Milton's memorial couplets on the " Marchioness of

(1) Poems of Milton, Ed. Masson, Vol. II, London, 1874, p. 332, 1.151. (2) 1.186. (3) Ed. cit., p. 424, 1639-40. (4) Ed. cit., p. 258, 1624. (5) 1624 Ed. cit., p. 258.

Winchester ",[1] or to his half-humorous, half-pathetic
lines on the " University Carrier ".[2] The verses on
Shakespeare[3] are more an epitaph than an elegy, but
his sonnet on his " Deceased Wife "[4] with its fair
vision and bitter awakening is a cry from the heart.
The elegiac poems of Milton are not, however, his
greatest achievement wherein lament for the
individual is forgotten in the tragical epic of fallen
humanity. Dryden, versatile poet though he was,
has left but few elegies, and among them there is
none which stands out as above the easy conventional eulogistic style of the age. They contain it is
true vigorous lines such as these from his " Ode to
the Memory of Mrs Anne Killigrew "[5]—

" When in mid-air the golden trump shall sound . . .
   The sacred poets first shall hear the sound,
   And foremost from the tomb shall bound,
   For they are covered with the lightest ground;
   And straight, with inborn vigour, on the wing,
   Like mounting larks, to the new morning sing ",[6]

and the couplet from " Eleonora "[7]—

" So softly death succeeded life in her,
   She did but dream of Heaven, and she was there "[8]

but it is vain to look for real feeling and emotion.
With Dryden the consideration of seventeenth century elegy may be closed. Looking back over this
period the number of memorial poems is no less striking than their similarity in treatment of subject.
" Personal elegy " became either a collection of artificial praises or an attempt to revive the convention
of the Pastoral, a form of poetry unsuited both to
sincerity and to simplicity of mourning. The few

(1) Ed. cit., p. 280, 1631. (2) Ed. cit., p. 278, 1631. (3) 1630. (4) 1656, Ed.
cit., p. 346. (5) and (6) Poems of Dryden, Globe Ed., 1870, p. 338, 1694. (7)
Ed. cit., p. 349 1692. (8) Ed. cit., p. 356.

exceptions mentioned make the easy flow and empty content of the majority more manifest.

The eighteenth century carried on the tradition and style of the late seventeenth, and " personal elegy " was still polished and artificial. Pope's " Elegy to the Memory of an Unfortunate Lady "[1] is typical of the finish and formality of this poet, but the ring of sincerity is absent. The same is true of Prior's verses on the " Death of the Queen "[2] and of those on " George Villiers ";[3] neither writer seems able to shake off the address to Gods or Muses, nor to avoid exaggerated apotheosis of his hero. Tickell's " Poem on Addison "[4] does not fulfil the author's own couplet—

> " Grief unaffected suits but ill with art,
> Or flowing numbers with a bleeding heart "[5]

for after an effective opening—

> " Can I forget the dismal night, that gave
> My soul's best part for ever to the grave ",[5]

the elegy wanders off into affected eulogy artistically presented. The " Letter to Tickell "[6] of Young, on the same subject, is similar in neatly-phrased adulation; speaking of the " Muse of Maro " he says—

> " Her finished charms to Addison she brings,
> Thinks in his thought and in his numbers sings.
> All read transported his pure classic page,
> Read and forget their climate and their age ".[7]

The great " Elegy Written in a Country Churchyard "[8] rises above the average poetry of the time

(1) Pope, " Poems ", 6 Vols, 1776, V. I, p. 137, 1720. (2) Prior, " Works ", 2 Vols., 1779, V. I, p. 49, 1695. (3) Ed. cit., V. I p. 194, 1703. (4) Works of Addison, 6 Vols., Ed. T. Tickell, 1804, V. I, p. xx. (5) Ed. cit., p. xx, 1721. (6) Poems of Young, 2 Vols., 1864, V. I, p. 336, 1719. (7) Ed. cit., p. 336. (8) 1751.

PERSONAL ELEGY IN ENGLISH POETRY.

in thought, reflection and expression, but as it is general in subject and not truly " personal ", in the objective sense defined earlier in this paper, it need not be considered here. Mention, however, must be made of Gray's Sonnet on the " Death of Richard West ".[1] This is more sincere than much eighteenth century work and has a fine conclusion—

" The fields to all their wonted tribute bear;
To warm their little loves the birds complain;
I fruitless mourn to him, that cannot hear,
And weep the more, because I weep in vain ".[2]

The panegyric on " Sir Isaac Newton ", by James Thomson,[3] is full of real enthusiasm for his subject, and sketches with no small skill the outline of the great mathematician's scientific discoveries; the finest and most " personal " lines are those which describe the character of a great seeker after knowledge—

" How greatly humble, how divinely good,
How firm establish'd on eternal truth;
Fervent in doing well, with every nerve
Still pressing on, forgetful of the past,
And panting for perfection; far above
Those little cares and visionary joys,
That so perplex the fond impassion'd heart
Of ever-cheated, ever-trusting man ".[4]

The same poet's tribute to Congreve[5] is less interesting in its conventional endowment of the dramatist with all the virtues of public and private life. Collins has left an "Ode " in quatrains on Thomson[6] which is more melodious than impressive—having the quiet finish and lack of vigour characteristic of this poet—

(1) Poems & Letters of T. Gray, Ed. W. Masson, 1820, p. 490. (2) Ed. cit., p. 490, 1768. (3) Works of James Thomson, 4 Vols., 1773, V. 2, p. 1. (4) p. 7, l.150. (5) Percy Soc., No. 35 1843. (6) Works of Collins, Aldine Ed., 1830, p. 63.

195

" Remembrance oft shall haunt the shore
    When Thames in summer wreaths is drest,
And oft suspend the dashing oar
    To bid his gentle spirit rest ".[1]

Thomas Warton's poem in memory of " Frederick, Prince of Wales "[2] is poor and artificial in extreme, but that of Chatterton[3] on " Thomas Phillips ",[4] in the metre of Gray's most famous poem, has many stanzas which, while over-praising and unfilled with deep emotion, have a pensive grace—

" Peace, gentlest, softest of the virtues, spread
    Her silver pinions, wet with dewy tears·
Upon her best distinguished poet's head
    And taught his lyre the music of the spheres ".[5]

Shenstone has left a collection of twenty-six "Elegies" with a prefatory Essay on this type of poem;[6] they are, however, neither remarkable for personal sorrow nor subject, and, while written in easy quatrains, are not above the average work of the time in this form of verse. Before passing to the elegiac work of Cowper and of Burns, wherein a new note of simplicity, pathos, and freedom from convention is struck, mention must be made of two other eighteenth century " personal " laments. The first is the poem of Johnson on the " Death of Robert Levet " which, although a little didactic in style, is evidently sincere. The last verse describes an ideal passing—

" Then with no fiery throbbing pain,
    No cold gradations of decay,
Death broke at once the vital chain
    And freed his soul the nearest way ".[7]

(1) p. 64, 1749.   (2) Works of T. Warton, Ed. R. Mant, Oxford, 1802, V. I, p. 24, 1751.   (3) Works of Chatterton, 2 Vols., 1875, V. I, p. 50.   (4) 1769. (5) 1769, p. 50.   (6) Works of Shenstone, 3 Vols., 1791, Vol. I.   (7) Oxford Book of English Verse, 1918, No. 451.

The second is the stanzas, " To Mary ", of Charles
Wolfe, whose more patriotic but less heart-felt
" Burial of Sir John Moore "[1] has brought him last-
ing fame.   There is much simple sorrow in these
lines—

> " If I had thought thou couldst have died,
>   I might not weep for thee;
> But I forgot when by thy side,
>   That thou couldst mortal be :
> It never through my mind had passed
>   The time could e'er be o'er,
> And I on thee should look my last,
>   And thou shouldst smile no more ".[2]

The chief elegiac poem of Cowper is his remembrance of his Mother called forth by her picture " sent
out of Norfolk ".   It is full of loneliness and a cruel
comparison between the happiness of childhood—

> " Thy nightly visits to my chamber made,
>   That thou mightst know me safe and warmly laid . . .
> All this, and more endearing still than all,
>   Thy constant flow of love . . ."[3]

and the misfortunes of manhood—

> " But me, scarce hoping to attain that rest,
>   Always from port witheld, always distressed,—
> Me howling blasts drive devious, tempest-tost,
> Sails ript, seams opening wide, and compass lost,
> And day by day some current's thwarting force
> Sets me more distant from a prosperous course ".[3]

A flame of suffering from the tragedy of this poet
lights these lines, and such a fire, had it been kindled
before, would have burnt up the conventionalities of
a Prior, a Warton, or a Shenstone.   Burns is not a

(1) O.B.E.V., No. 603.   (2) O.B.E.V., No. 604.   (3) Cowper, Poems, Ed.
Willmott, 1855, p. 403, 1790.

great elegist. His pathetic " Bard's Epitaph " is really on himself, and so outside the objective treatment of this paper. There is, however, a tender charm in the lines—

> " The mother-linnet in the brake
>   Bewails her ravished young;
> So I, for my lost darling's sake,
>   Lament the live-day long.
> Death, oft I've feared thy fatal blow,
>   Now, fond I bare my breast;
> Oh do thou kindly lay me low
>   With him I love, at rest ",[1]

which contain greater emotion than the more elaborate laments on " James Hunter Blair "[2] and on " Robert Dundas ".[3] The simple verse of Cowper and of Burns marks the coming of a new spirit into English elegy, a spirit wherein the " personal note " is sincere and the imagery, if used, linked with the subject of the poem. It becomes a carefully entwined wreath of remembrance, rather than a collection of scattered leaves, and a tribute worthy the dead to whom it is offered.

The nineteenth century elegy, which now claims attention, is only one form of poetry in an age which is the richest of our literature, but that it could achieve perfect melody, restraint, and yet deep feeling, is shown by " Adonais ",[4] " In Memoriam ",[5] " Thyrsis "[6] and " Ave atque Vale ",[7] the four greatest poems in this style. Before passing on to these, however, reference may be made to the work of some other poets, although in their cases, such verse was not often chosen as a medium. Wordsworth, Coleridge, and Southey, have left few poems

(1) Poems of Burns, 1892, pp. 475, 100. (2) Ed. cit., p. 86. (3) Ed. cit., p. 95. (4) 1821. (5) 1850. (6) 1861. (7) 1867?

which can be called true " personal laments ", while
Keats and Moore have left none. Of the first three
writers, Wordsworth's " Poet's Epitaph "[1] is akin to
that of Burns on the same subject, while his more
striking " Poems at the Grave " of the Scotch singer[2]
are filled with reflective melancholy; a stanza may
be given—

> " And oh for Thee, by pitying grace
> Checked oft-times in a devious race,
> May He, who halloweth the place
>   Where man is laid,
> Receive thy Spirit in the embrace
>   For which it prayed ".[3]

His lines in memory of his Brother who was drowned
in 1805[4] do not reach the beauty of the other portrait
in " The Happy Warrior ",[5] but there is real affection in those on Lamb, himself the author of a delicate lament on " An Infant dying as soon as Born ".[6]
Some of Wordsworth's tribute may be quoted—

> " To a good man of most dear memory
> This stone is sacred . . .
> Affections, warm as sunshine, free as air;
> And when the precious hours of leisure came,
> Knowledge and wisdom, gained from converse sweet
> With books, or while he ranged the crowded streets
> With a keen eye, and overflowing heart.
> So genius triumphed over seeming wrong
> And poured out truth in work by thoughtful love
> Inspired, works potent over smiles and tears ".[7]

To these may be added the deep-felt stanzas on
" James Hogg "[8] with their reference to Coleridge—

(1) Poems of Wordsworth; Ed. W. Knight, London, 1904, p. 430. (2) Ed. cit.,
pp. 210, 213. (3) Ed. cit., p. 212. (4) Ed. cit., p. 502. (5) Ed. cit., p. 444.
(6) Poetical Works of C. Lamb, London, 1838 p. 182. (7) Wordsworth, Ed.
cit., p. 306. (8) Ed. cit., p. 510.

" Nor has the rolling year twice measured
From sign to sign, its steadfast course
Since every mortal power of Coleridge
Was frozen at its marvellous source "[1]

whose " Monody on the Death of Chatterton "[2] is a
powerful and imaginative memorial to " The sleepless
soul that perished in its pride "[3] of whom he says—

" Yet will I love to follow the sweet dream . . .
And on some hill, whose forest-frowning side
Waves o'er the murmurs of his calmer tide,
Will raise a solemn Cenotaph to thee,
Sweet Harper of time-shrouded Minstrelsy ".[4]

Southey, to whom Wordsworth has addressed the
lines—

" The vales and hills whose beauty hither drew
The poet's steps, and fixed him here, on you
His eyes have closed . . ."[5]

has left but one "elegiac poem " which need be mentioned here, his beautiful " The Dead Friend "[6]—

" Not to the grave, not to the grave, my Soul,
Follow thy friend beloved,
But in the lonely hour,
But in the evening walk,
Think that he companies thy solitude,
Think that he holds with thee
Mysterious intercourse;
And though remembrance wake a tear
There will be joy in grief ".[7]

Byron has also an " Epitaph on a Friend ",[8] but it
is less sincere than that just quoted. Many of his

(1) Ed. cit., p. 510. (2) Poems of S. T. Coleridge, 3 Vols., London, 1835,
Vol. I, p. 7. (3) Wordsworth, Ed. cit., p. 124. (4) Coleridge, Ed. cit., p. 12.
(5) Wordsworth, Ed. cit., p. 511. (6) Southey, Poet. Works, London 1850, p.
131. (7) 1799. (8) Byron, Poems, London, 1866, p. 4.

poems indeed are tinged with the pathos of elegy,
but few have the scope and the dignity which are
the mark of the greatest " personal laments ".
Dignity is certainly a characteristic of Scott's lines in
memory of Nelson, Pitt, and Fox; with their fine
conclusion—

> " The solemn echo seems to cry,
> ' Here let their discord with them die,
> Speak not for those a separate doom
> Whom Fate made Brothers in the tomb ".[1] [2]

Leaving the elegiac work, if any, of other less important early nineteenth century poets, the great hymn
to the spirit of Keats, Shelley's " Adonais ", may be
approached. This wonderful poem ever humbles the
critic who nears its melodious beauty and glorious
imagery, for the very Spirits of Nature—

> " All he had loved, and moulded into thought,
> From shape, and hue, and odour, and sweet sound,
> Lamented Adonais. Morning sought
> Her eastern watch-tower, and her hair unbound,
> Wet with the tears which should adorn the ground;
> Dimmed the aerial eyes that kindle day;
> Afar the melancholy thunder moaned,
> Pale ocean in unquiet slumber lay,
> And the wild winds flew round, sobbing in their
>   dismay ".[3]

Very reverently, for fear of sacrilege, and in memory
of the dead singer, may it be pointed out how his
"most musical of mourners"[4] wove together the lovely
laments of Bion and of Moschus[5] (which he himself
partially translated)[6] reviving and re-awakening
the form of weeping Cytherea[7] and the sad echo of the

(1) and (2) Poems of Sir W. Scott, London, 1906, " Marmion ", p. 89. (3)
Shelley's Poetical Works, Ed. by H. Buxton Forman, 5 Vols., 1892, " Adonais ",
St. XIV. (4) " Adonais ", St. IV. (5) " Theocritus, Bion & Moschus " Trans.
A. Lang, 1920, p. 173, 198. (6) Shelley, Wks., Ed. cit., Vol. 5, p. 202. (7)
Ed. cit. Bion, Idyll I.

rocks.[1] Marvelling also as the " one frail Form "[2] voices his sorrow through the haunting measure of the Spenserian verse, kin to the earlier poet in music but passing from his allegory to thoughts that

> " along that rugged way,
> Pursued, like raging hounds, their father and their prey ".[3]

the hearer is carried upward from the world of decay and joined with Nature, Adonais and " The inheritors of unfulfilled renown "[4] those who " Rose from their thrones " to greet the hierophant of beauty and of truth. He is—

> " borne darkly, fearfully, afar;
> Whilst burning through the inmost veil of Heaven,
> The soul of Adonais, like a star,
> Beacons from the abode where the Eternal are "[5]

for the mortal is clothed with immortality. Verily the lines of Plato (?) are true of this seer of visions and dreamer of dreams, and not in-fortunately are they placed on the title-page of this elegy—

> " Thou wert the morning star among the living,
>   Ere thy fair light had fled;—
> Now, having died, thou art as Hesperus, giving
>   New splendour to the dead ".[6]

Yet Shelley, while rousing Nature to mourn with him, did not forget the pathos of human parting—

> " What form leans sadly o'er the white death-bed,
>   In mockery of monumental stone,
> The heavy heart heaving without a moan?
> If it be He, who, gentlest of the wise,
> Taught, soothed, loved, honoured the departed one,
> Let me not vex with inharmonious sighs
> The silence of that heart's accepted sacrifice "[7]

(1) Ed. cit. Moschus, Idyll III. (2) " Adonais ", St. XXXI. (3) " Adonais ", St. XXXI. (4) " Adonais ", St. XLV. (5) " Adonais ", St. LV. (6) Shelley, Wks., Ed. cit., Vol. V, p. 200. (7) " Adonais ", St. XXXV.

nor even does the poem " with imagination all compact " become impersonal. Glorified by the harmony
of verse, the loss of the young poet and " the pity
of it " is in his mind; and it is no vague complaint
but bitter scorn which fills the denunciation—

" Remorse and Self-contempt shall cling to thee;
Hot Shame shall burn upon thy secret brow,
And like a beaten hound tremble thou shalt—as now ".[1]

" Adonais " is a sublime elegy, for it has the power
of perfect poetry, it is a real lament, for it is dedi-
cated to the unfulfilled promise of John Keats. Walter
Savage Landor, who wrote—

" Shelley whose song so sweet was sweetest here,
We knew each other little; now I walk
Along the same green path, along the shore
Of Lerici . . ."[2]

has not left any definite " personal elegy ", although
many of his short miscellaneous poems are very
pathetic and the lovely lines to " The Sister of Elia "
on her brother—

" He leaves behind him freed from griefs and years
Far worthier things than tears;
The love of friends without a single foe
Unequalled lot below "[3]

must not be forgotten. With the " In Memoriam "
of Tennyson, the second great nineteenth century
elegy is reached; and its beauty as an expression of
personal emotion must be considered. There is some
guidance for the writer on this most wonderful poem
in the divisions made by the author, who said that
the groups of stanzas, although composed at various
times and at different places, were separated in their

(1) " Adonais ", St. XXXVII. (2) Landor, " Last Fruit off an Old Tree ",
1853, p. 449. (3) Wks. of Landor, 2 Vols., 1846, Vol. 2, p. 673.

aspect of the loss by the Christmas festivals. The first is that of brooding sorrow—

" At our old pastimes in the hall
    We gambol'd, making vain pretence
    Of gladness, with an awful sense
Of one mute Shadow watching all.

We paused : the winds were in the beech;
    We heard them sweep the winter land;
    And in a circle hand-in-hand
Sat silent, looking each at each "[1]

the second of resignation—

" Again at Christmas did we weave
    The holly round the Christmas hearth,
    The silent snow possess'd the earth,
And calmly fell our Christmas eve ";[2]

the third of peaceful recollection and, on his birthday, of fellowship—

" Bring in great logs and let them lie,
    To make a solid core of heat;
    Be cheerful-minded, talk and treat
Of all things ev'n as he were by ";[3]

The death of his fellow-student and friend made a far deeper impression on Tennyson than that of his college companion and comrade on Milton. The loss of Arthur Hallam was a heart-break, of Edward King a passing sorrow. It is the depth from which it sprang and the tears with which it was watered that gives the haunting fragrance to the song-flower planted on the grave at Clevedon. " In Memoriam ", as a study of Tennyson's battle with grief, doubt and fear, is outside the scope of this paper, but whatever his opinions on evolution, philosophy and deity,

(1) " In Memoriam ", Golden Treasury Series, London, 1892, St. XXX. (2) Ed. cit., St. LXXVIII. (3) Ed. cit., St. CVII.

over the whole poem rises the spirit to whom he
prays—

> " Be near me when my light is low,
>   When the blood creeps, and the nerves prick
>   And tingle; and the heart is sick,
> And all the wheels of Being slow ".[1]

It is, however, the stanzas which describe Hallam as
the friend and companion in the days past when the
poet says—

> " By night we linger'd on the lawn,
>   For underfoot the herb was dry;
>   And genial warmth; and o'er the sky
> The silvery haze of summer drawn "[2]

and the miss of his actual presence, which form the
elegiac key-notes of the poem; they are often indeed
struck through the earlier verses, while this group
sounds them both in lovely lines—

> " The path by which we twain did go,
>   Which led by tracts that pleased us well,
>   Thro' four sweet years arose and fell,
> From flower to flower, from snow to snow;
>
> And we with singing cheer'd the way,
>   And, crown'd with all the season lent,
>   From April on to April went,
> And glad at heart from May to May;
>
> But where the path we walk'd began
>   To slant the fifth autumnal slope,
>   As we descended following Hope,
> There sat the Shadow fear'd of man;
>
> Who broke our fair companionship,
>   And spread his mantle dark and cold,
>   And wrapt thee formless in the fold,
> And dull'd the murmur on thy lip,

(1) Ed. cit., St. L.   (2) Ed. cit., St. XCV.

> And bore thee where I could not see
> Nor follow, tho' I walk in haste,
> And think, that somewhere in the waste
> The Shadow sits and waits for me ".[1]

One of the mysteries of " In Memoriam " is the genius
of the poet in weaving his thought through the glories
of Nature, with which each mood finds sympathy;
and this glory is the beauty of England, not of an
imaginary world like that surrounding the tragedy
of " Adonais " but—

> " 'Tis well; 'tis something; we may stand
> Where he in English earth is laid,
> And from his ashes may be made
> The violet of his native land ".[2]

It is this link with reality and this accuracy of
description which is one of the great differences
between the elegy of Shelley and that of Tennyson—
the one calls on the spirit of Nature to mourn with
him, the other finds refreshment for his own spirit in
her calm or storm. " In Memoriam " lacks the
magnificent visions of " Adonais " but it holds a
power of cameo-like carving, of peace—

> " Calm and still light on yon great plain
> That sweeps with all its autumn bowers,
> And crowded farms and lessening towers,
> To mingle with the bounding main ";[3]

and of unrest—

> " The forest crack'd, the waters curl'd,
> The cattle huddled on the lea;
> And wildly dash'd on tower and tree
> The sunbeam strikes along the world ".[4]

(1) Ed. cit., St. XXII. (2) Ed. cit., St. XVIII. (3) Ed. cit., St. XI. (4) Ed. cit., St. XV.

In Shelley's world the dead poet becomes the " Son of Urania and a beacon to Eternty ", but in that of Tennyson, his friend is never far off from his life. Hence it is that " In Memoriam " is more personal than " Adonais " and in the simple sincerity of grief, if not in ethereal beauty, the greater elegy. The " Ode on the Death of the Duke of Wellington "[1] is the only other long memorial poem left by Tennyson, and fine though it be in the mingling of national grief and patriotism, it is written by a poet voicing the emotion of a people, and with them his own; it is not the cry of a saddened and perplexed heart for a beloved friend. It is a great poem rising to a noble conclusion—

> " He is gone who seem'd so great—
>   Gone, but nothing can bereave him
>   Of the force he made his own
>   Being here, and we believe him
>   Something far advanced in State,
>   And that he wears a truer crown
>   Than any wreath that man can weave him,
>   Speak no more of his renown,
>   Lay your earthly fancies down,
>   And in the vast cathedral leave him,
>   God accept him, Christ receive him ",[2]

but it does not reveal the real genius of the poet; there is more pathos in one of the above-quoted stanzas from " In Memoriam " than in these sonorous and processional lines. There is more of heart in these lines from the poem on "The Death of the Duke of Clarence "—

(1) Works of Tennyson, London, 1899, 1 Vol.   (2) p. 218, 1852.

" The face of Death is toward the Sun of Life,
His shadow darkens earth; his truer name
Is ' Onward ', no discordance in the roll
And march of that Eternal Harmony
Whereto the worlds beat time, tho' faintly heard
Until the great Hereafter. Mourn in hope ! "[1]

With thse thoughts, which are also the soul of " In
Memoriam " the consideration of Tennyson's elegiac
work may be concluded. It is strange that neither
Robert Browning nor his wife left any outstanding
tributes to the dead. There is indeed true pathos
in the former's " Evelyn Hope "[2] but it has hardly
the structure of an " elegy ", while among the poems
of Mrs Browning, the spirit of mourning over a poet
is voiced by " Cowper's Grave "[3] and over a child by
the tender simplicity of the " Grave at Florence ".[4]
It is not, however, until the work of Matthew Arnold
is reached that another great elegy calls for mention.
The " Thyrsis "[5] of this poet is a beautiful tribute
to the poet Clough, who died at Florence in 1861,
but it, like " In Memoriam ", whose inspiration also
passed away beyond these shores, is filled with
English flower scents and memories. " The Scholar
Gipsy ", published thirteen years earlier, preludes this
rich lament, and the recollections of the wanderer
and the friend mingle in the calm and solemn stanzas.
Is it fanciful to imagine that if Keats had ever written
an " elegy " it would have been a forerunner of
" Thyrsis ", for the magic of this poem is akin to
that of the " Ode to Autumn "? And yet perhaps
this very loveliness of painting lessens the pathos of
personal loss, and the poet recalls the scene rather
than the subject of his poem. The monody is sincere

(1) Ed. cit., p. 894, 1889. (2) Poems of Browning, Oxford Ed., 1905, p. 13.
(3) E. B. Browning. Works. 5 Vols., London, 1877, Vol. III, p. 116. (4)
Ed. cit., p. 164. (5) 1866.

and deeply felt, but it seeks refuge from pain in the memory of old haunts and in the opiate of Nature. And if Nature is the healer now, it would have been so to his friend while he lived, for the stanza addressing the cuckoo could have been applied to him—

" Too quick despairer, wherefore wilt thou go?
    Soon will the high Midsummer pomps come on,
    Soon will the musk carnations break and swell,
    Soon shall we have gold-dusted snapdragon,
    Sweet-William with his homely cottage-smell,
        And stocks in fragrant blow;
    Roses that down the alleys shine afar,
        And open, jasmine-muffled lattices,
    And groups under the dreaming garden-trees,
    And the full moon, and the white evening-star ".[1]

The poem is full of lines which create an image whose vivid clearness is unforgettable, as—

" Where are the mowers, who, as the tiny swell
        Of our boat passing heav'd the river grass,
        Stood with suspended scythe to see us pass?
    They all are gone, and thou art gone as well ! "[2]

It is indeed a wonderful example of " emotion recollected in tranquility ", and is free from the stress of everyday problems. In the fields round his beloved Oxford Arnold found the peace he sought on the death of his friend and an atmosphere of tender melancholy is over this restrained and musical " elegy ". " Thyrsis " is not, however, the only personal lament of this poet. There are the sensitive lines " By a Deathbed "[3]—

(1) Poems of M. Arnold, Oxford, 1909; p. 388; " Thyrsis " St. 7. (2) Ed. cit., p. 389, St. 13. (3) M. Arnold, Poems, Ed. cit., p. 139, 1852.

> " But ah, though peace indeed is here,
>   And ease from shame, and rest from fear;
>   Though nothing can dismarble now
>   The smoothness of that limpid brow;
>   Yet is a calm like this in truth,
>   The crowning end of life and youth? "[1]

and the reflective " Memorial Verses "[2] to Goethe,
Byron, and Wordsworth. There is indeed a statuesque
quality in the poetry of Arnold, admirably fitted for
elegiac composition, and it is strange that he has not
left more poems in this form. Passing over the work
of the Rossettis', although not forgetting the Sonnets
of Gabriel on Chatterton, Blake, Coleridge, Keats and
Shelley,[3] nor the beautiful simplicity of faith in the
verse of his sister Christina, and her lovely lines—

> " Remember me when I am gone away
>   Gone far away into the silent land . . .
>   Better by far you should forget and smile,
>   Than that you should remember, and be sad "[4]

leaving also the poetry of William Morris who was
not an elegist; the " Ave atque Vale " of Swinburne
may be considered. This fine poem to the memory of
Charles Baudelaire, from whose " Fleurs du Mal "
(1857) the prefatory quotation is taken—

" Nous devrions pourtant lui porter quelques fleurs;
Les morts, les pauvres morts, ont de grandes douleurs"[5]

is the flower tribute of an English poet to the genius
of a French singer, whose gift was akin to his own.
It has the richness of melody which is characteristic
of Swinburne's verse, but it does not perhaps give
the reader a sense of passionate grief. It has the
vision of " Adonais " without its ecstasy, and the
music of " Thyrsis " without its calm. Lovely as are

(1) p. 139. (2) Ed. cit., p. 162, 1850. (3) Poems of D. G. Rossetti, 2 Vols.,
London, 1904, Vol. II, p. 29. (4) Poetical Works of C. Rossetti, 1914, p. 294,
1849. (5) Baudelaire 1821-1867.

many of the stanzas, as that wherein the living poet
seeks answer from the dead—

" Hast thou found any likeness for thy vision ?
O gardener of strange flowers, what bud, what bloom,
Hast thou found sown, what gathered in the gloom ?
What of despair, of rapture, of derision,
What of life is there, what of ill or good ?
Are the fruits grey like dust or bright like blood ?
Does the dim ground grow any seed of ours,
The faint fields quicken any terrene root,
In low lands where the sun and moon are mute
And all the stars keep silence ?   Are there flowers
    At all, or any fruit ? "[1]

they hold a strange feverish unrest and, while filling
the mind with subtle harmonies and minor chords, do
not wake the most vital notes of the heart. It is a
wonderful poem, but not a great " personal elegy ";
a beautifully wrought wreath, but of hot-house
blossoms. Magical in its flowing melody, when read
the sound haunts the ear but not the thought the
spirit. The appeal to the ear rather than the cry to
the spirit is indeed characteristic of many tributes
paid by Swinburne to the dead. The rolling lines of
the memorial to " Barry Cornwall "—

" In the garden of death, where the singers whose names
    are deathless
One with another make music unheard of men,
Where the dead sweet roses fade not of lips long breath-
    less,
And the fair eyes shine that shall weep not or change
    again,
Who comes now crowned with the blossom of snow-white
    years ?
What music is this that the world of the dead men
    hears ? "[2]

(1) Selections from A. C. Swinburne, Ed. Gosse & Wise, 1919, p. 164.   (2)
Ed. cit., p. 173, 1874.

the hymns on the centenary of Landor[1] and the
festival of Victor Hugo[2] have the gorgeous harmonies
and finished form of this singer, but the voice of
tender regret and of simple pathos is too often absent.
But Swinburne did possess this voice, and his stanzas
on "A Baby's Death "[3] are some of the most perfect
he ever wrote, for they ring true in emotion and
grief—

> " The little hands that never sought
> Earth's prizes, worthless all as sands,
> What gift has death, God's servant, brought
>   The little hands?
> We ask; but love's self silent stands,
> Love, that lends eyes and wings to thought
> To search where death's dim heaven expands.
> Ere this, perchance, though love know nought,
> Flowers fill them, grown in lovelier lands,
> Where hands of guiding angels caught
>   The little hands ".

With these lines it may be well to close this study
of nineteenth century elegy; but no writer on this
subject can afford to forget the beautiful memorial
poetry of two more modern elegists. The verses of
Robert Bridges, " On a Dead Child "[4] have the tenderness of the last quoted lines of Swinburne, and also
kinship with the earlier laments of Milton and of
Lamb—

> " So quiet—doth the change content thee?   Death,
>   whither hath he taken thee?
> To a world, do I think, that rights the disaster
>   of this?
>   The vision of which I miss,
> Who weep for the body, and wish but to warm thee
>   and awaken thee? "[4]

(1) Swinburne, " Studies in Song ", 1880, 1864.   (2) Swinburne, " Songs of
the Springtides ", 1880.   (3) Ed. cit., p. 202.   (4) Poetical Works of Bridges,
Oxford, 1912, Poems, Bk. III, p. 267, 1890.

while there is haunting pathos in—

> " I never shall love the snow again
>   Since Maurice died;
> With corniced drift it blocked the lane
> And sheeted in a desolate plain
>   The country side ".[1]

Nor is his more elaborate " Elegy on a lady whom
grief for the death of her betrothed killed "[2] lacking
solemnity, the last stanza—

> " And thou, O lover, that art on the watch,
>   Where, on the banks of the forgetful streams,
>   The pale indifferent ghosts wander, and snatch
> The sweeter moments of their broken dreams,—
>   Thou, when the torchlight gleams,
>   When thou shalt see the slow procession,
>   And when thine ears the fitful music catch,
>   Rejoice, for thou art near to thy possession "[2]

gives the personal loss a new aspect mingling hope
and sorrow. The other elegist to whom reference
must be made is Sir William Watson. His poems in
memory of Burns,[3] Wordsworth,[4] and Arnold,[5] are
full of beautiful sincerity of feeling, and his verses
for the " Centenary of Shelley "[6] catch the very
spirit of his

> " Wild odours shaken from strange wings,
>   And unfamiliar whisperings
>   From far lips blown ".[7]

But there is no more fitting conclusion to these pages
than the final lines of his restrained, melancholy, but
wonderful " Lacrimae Musarum "[8] and these lines of

(1) Ed. cit., Bk. V, p. 309, 1894. (2) Ed. cit., Bk. I, p. 238, 1890. (3)
Poems of William Watson, 2 Vols., 1905, " Tomb of Burns ". (4) " Wordsworth's
Grave ". (5) In Laleham Churchyard. (6) " Lacrimae Musarum ", 1893, p. 41,
1892. (7) St. 17. (8) Ed. cit., p. 9, 1892.

one great poet on another may well haunt the ear
for ever—

" The seasons change, the winds they shift and veer,
     The grass of yesteryear
Is dead; the birds depart, the groves decay,
Empires dissolve, and peoples disappear
     Song passes not away.
Captains and conquerors leave a little dust,
And kings a dubious legend of their reign,
   The swords of Cæsars they are less than rust,
   The poet doth remain ".

  .   .   .   .

The nineteenth century is so rich in elegy that it is
impossible to do more than touch on some of the
most representative poems; and while there would
probably be little difference of opinion on the choice
of the four greatest, of those less known, but possibly
no less well loved, it is hard to choose the best. In
retrospect, however, the great characteristics of the
nineteenth century " personal objective elegy "
appear to be perfect freedom of form, a rich music and
an imaginative vision, linked with deep admiration,
hope, faith and love. Each approach to the problem
of death is from a different standpoint, and yet each
poet in his own way asserts the supremacy of the
spirit and realises that the tomb is not the end of
existence nor of beauty.

  Is not this the true ideal before every writer of
" personal elegy "? The poet has not sometimes, as
in the seventeenth and eighteenth centuries, risen
above the eulogy of his friend and hero, although
earlier periods may have given him examples of
deeper emotion, but even so his tribute to another

life has value. How much more then in the greater spiritual elegies of later years, when the cruelty of death and the praise of nobility are mingled with the themes of hope and faith in reunion, does the glory of poetry voice the vision of futurity and the grave become but the gateway to immortality !

" Finis coronat opus ".

BIOGRAPHY, ITS USE AND ABUSE.

A Paper read before the " Gwynant " Society of Hampstead. May, 1922.

BIOGRAPHY, ITS USE AND ABUSE.

EVERY biographer would be wise to remember the remark of Oliver Wendel Holmes that there are always three personalities in humanity. " The real John, known only to his Maker, John's ideal John, never the real one, and often very unlike him, Thomas' ideal John, never the real John, nor John's John, but often very unlike either ". No one can write the life of the first John, only John himself that of the second John, and only Thomas that of the third John. It is the estimate of Thomas which is important in biography; and the success or failure of his work will depend upon his sympathy with or antipathy to his subject. Moreover, since it is impossible to be certain that either the like or dislike of Thomas is fundamentally just, his biography can never be really accurate. So we are reduced to the conclusion that all biographical writing is only an approximation to the truth. Every work of this nature resolves itself into an attempt to create an impression of a character; and this attempt may be made from two bases; one founded on the belief that the age influences the person, and the other on the belief that the person influences the age. The biographer holding the former premise will strive to give his readers a clear vision of the period in which his subject lived, and to achieve this will concentrate on historical data, contemporary opinion and general environment. Having, as it were, painted the background of his picture, he will place the character which he is studying in the foreground, and move away to contemplate the general effect, returning to correct the perspective or proportion. The author who undertakes biography on the latter system will adopt another scheme. Searching out all the available material that personally concerns his subject, he will outline his form and character with vigorous strokes, and having created a portrait, vivify it and see the figure moving about among his fellowmen, and exercising a good or evil influence upon the time in which he lives. A good example of the first type is furnished by the " Life of Milton " by Masson, or to give it its full title "The Life of John Milton; narrated in connection with the Political, Ecclesiastical and Literary History of his Time ", by David Masson, M.D., LL.D., etc. It is to this book that Lowell refers when he says: " It is plain from the preface to the second volume (and there are six large tomes !) that Mr Masson himself has an uneasy consciousness that something is wrong, and that Milton ought somehow to be more than a mere incident of his own biography ! ". Here, then, is the danger which besets a biographer of this type, the risk of too much external information and of too little concentration on the person with whom he deals. It must, however, be said, in justice to Mr Masson, that his work is a most comprehensive history of the greater part of the seventeenth century ! Perhaps the most famous model of the second, or personal, form of biography, is the " Life of Johnson ". Here the whole energy of Boswell is used to give a picture of the Doctor, as he had known him; and there is much truth in the remark of Sir Edward Cook that " He (Boswell) had an instinct for what was interesting and characteristic ". Yet this form has also its dangers, it may so easily became a mere flattery or a skilful misrepresentation. An example of the first is given in Dowden's "Life of Shelley", which, although a favourite with lovers of the poet, is not an impartial judgment; and of the second, which is fortunately the rarer, the "Life of Johnson", by Macaulay. This indeed shows the misuse of a fine art and is not difficult to discover and condemn; but the unduly favourable account is no less unjust, though far more insidious. So many considerations enter into the estimate of a life by one who was deeply interested in, or closely attached to, the person. Family pride and over-emphasis on particular attributes, as in Hallam's "Life of Tennyson"; insufficiency of study as in Mrs Gaskell's "Life of Charlotte Brontë"; too frequent quotation from correspondence as in Cross' "Life of George Eliot"; a desire in the writer to justify his subject in some opinion, founded on his own adherence to it, as in Bacon's "Life of Henry VIIth"; and perhaps most subtle of all, a wish to show how brilliantly the biographer himself can write upon somebody else, as in a modern "Life of Browning". Such are a few of the dangers which harass the biographer, and considering them, it is reasonable to ask, where shall the truth be found? Nor can refuge be taken in the comforting aphorism "Many biographies are better than one history", for this breaks down in the consideration of a world-wide personality, such as Napoleon. The life of this general by Rose is as much history as biography, and "Napoleon, the last Phase", by Rosebery, more biography than history. New difficulties, moreover, arise, for the student is faced by many histories and innumerable biographies; there are lives of politicians, generals, admirals, poets and musicians, and whenever a new fact is discovered concerning them, a fresh biographer is at hand to record it. Would it not be wiser to follow the suggestion of Mr George Santayana stated thus in his paragraphs " Against Prying Biographers ": " Our ignorance of the life of a great writer is not, I think, much to be regretted. His work preserves that part of him which he himself would have wished to preserve . . . where intelligence is attained, the rest of a man, like the scaffolding to a finished building, becomes irrelevant. We do not wish it to intercept our view of the solid structure which was alone intended by the artist ". Perhaps so, but it would mean the loss of an environment and the neglect of an important modulative force. It appears, therefore, that some biographical details are necessary, and the question turns on their relative values, which again depend upon the estimate made by the writer, an estimate which may be sincere but erroneous, mistaken yet of good intent.

We are now faced with another problem : Is the man who has his life written during his life-time more fortunate than he who is judged after his death ? If he be alive he can contradict his biographer, and if dead, a friend will, in another biography, do it for him ! Hence families of lives and lives of families ! Moreover, is either critic or eulogist sincere ? Although many would reply in the negative, it must be remembered that the first author in the field will be nearest to his subject, and will be certainly sincere in his admiration, for unless he admired he would not write; and that the second may be sincere in considering his criticism justified by fact and not by favour. A modern example is given by Sir George Arthur's "Life of Lord Kitchener " and by the " corrected impression " (or depression ?) of the same character by

BIOGRAPHY, ITS USE AND ABUSE.

Viscount Esher. They are both written with sincerity, but it is history alone that can judge which is the more true.

There is, however, one means of escape from these problems, and that apparently simple. " Let the man or woman write his or her own life ; they at least know the facts ". But what a strain this throws on the individual judgment ! It presupposes that the public want to know about him, and quite as often, about her, an assumption hard to reconcile with humility, and implies either pretended self-diffidence or gives scope to personal rancour. Auto-biography is a dangerous literary gamble. But like many others the gamble sometimes succeeds, and a good auto-biography traces the growth of a mind from within and not, as a biography, from without, contains more originality if less accuracy than an external account, and is of more interest to the psychologist than to the historian. The author cannot, however, carry his story to its natural conclusion, for, as Thomas Hood wittily writes in his " Death's Ramble "—

" He saw an author writing his life,
   But he let him write no further ;
For Death who strikes whenever he likes
   Is jealous of all self-murther ! "

In spite, however, of the lack of finality in his tale, there is indeed one great advantage to be gained by the auto-biographist ; the certainty of one friend—himself—outweighing in his eyes the existence of one enemy—his first critic—probably mentioned in the life, and feeling it incumbent upon him to re-state an incident " as it really occurred ". We must not, therefore, expect too much of an auto-biography ; it may have sincerity, charm and frankness, but can never equal the balanced estimate of external critics; for the mean of their various interpretations, individually favourable or hostile, will probably be nearer the truth. So far we have mentioned the honest attempt of a writer to give an account of his own life; but besides this type of auto-biography there is that which " Punch " succinctly calls " nauto-biography" which may be defined as "writing one's own life in order to miswrite that of another ". In other words, there are auto-biographies that depend for their interest or appeal on the feeling of unkind curiosity about the affairs of others, a feeling which to judge by the work of some modernists is unfortunately growing. It is certainly a grave misuse of an art to employ it for an ignoble purpose, and in a wish to be brilliant to be irreverent. Reverence, reticence and restraint are the keynotes of good biography, and even more of honest auto-biography; reverence for the lives of others, reticence on selfish interests, and restraint in judgment and opinion.

The mention of this triple standard brings us to the question of personal correspondence. Should it, or should it not, be included in the life of its writer? Both views can be supported. Lovers of Keats considered the publication of the Brawne letters, unfortunate and unfair to the poet by and to whom they were written, arguing that while his communications with literary contemporaries were important as throwing light upon his works, his private writings and thoughts had better remain unread; and it is quite true that some critics and biographers seem to belong to the class who would steal jewels from a tomb and use their material with as little consideration as the thieves their treasure. On the other hand, the psychologists maintain that it is in these most sacred and personal records that the greatest sincerity lies, as they were written trusting that no other eye than one would read them; holding it necessary for a complete understanding of the author's character that every detail should be revealed. It is, of course, true that environment is more important in some cases than in others. One is entitled to ask whether Johnson did not gain his position as leader of a literary circle more by his words than by his works; and Shelley his neglect as a poet, more by his life than by his lyrics. In the former case an estimate of personality and of setting is of far more importance than in the latter. Once again, therefore, we are forced back to the position that everything depends on the spirit of the biographer. Assuming that he has the facts at his command he is responsible for concealment and revelation. If he remember to be thorough yet not petty, careful yet not meticulous, just yet not unmerciful, he will create a fine example of a noble art used for a high purpose; if he neglect research and judgment, patience and loyalty, feeling and sincerity, he will but mis-employ a wonderful opportunity for service, in the pursuit of transient gain. Everyone could mention biographies which reach the former or the latter standard; in an age of psychology, such as the present, both abound.

In conclusion, turn once more to the words of Holmes. " Every person's feelings ", he writes, " have a front-door and a side-door by which they may be entered. The front-door is on the street. Some keep it always open; some keep it latched; some locked; some bolted with a chain that will let you peep in but not get in; and some nail it up, so that nothing can pass its threshold. This front-door leads into a passage which opens into an ante-room, and this into the interior apartments. The side-door opens at once into the sacred chambers ". It is not necessary for the biographer to enter the " sacred chambers ", at least until after the death of the householder, and even then the entrance should be reverent. There must be an end to iconoclastic methods, to the writer who bursts into the " interior apartments " seizing and crying, " I have found his hidden treasure, let me sell it for my profit ". Truly the words of Lincoln apply to biography as to life, " With malice towards none, with charity for all, with firmness in the right, as God gives us to see the right; let us strive to finish the work we are engaged in ". The use or abuse of biography is the true or false interpretation of this ideal.

Date Due

FORM 109